A Sequential Program for Adults

Book Four

Program Authors

Linda Ward Beech • **James W. Beers**
Jo Ann Dauzat • **Sam V. Dauzat** • **Tara McCarthy**

Program Consultants

David C. Bub
Albany-Schoharie-Schenectady B.O.C.E.S.
Albany, New York

Christina H. Miller
Shoals Area Adult Education Program
Muscle Shoals, Alabama

Dannette S. Queen
Office of Adult and Continuing Education
New York, New York

John Ritter
Oregon Women's Correctional Center
Salem, Oregon

Lydia Smith
Adult Literacy Instructors' Training Institute
Los Angeles, California

Betty L. Walker
Richard J. Daley College
Chicago, Illinois

STECK-VAUGHN
C O M P A N Y
A Subsidiary of National Education Corporation

Acknowledgments

● ● ● ● ●

Staff Credits:

Executive Editor:	Ellen Lehrburger
Senior Supervising Editor:	Carolyn Hall
Project Editor:	Margie Weaver
Design Manager:	Donna Brawley
Electronic Production:	Kristian Polo, Shelly Knapp
Cover Design:	Pamela Heaney
Photo Editor:	Margie Foster

Photography Credits: pp. 6, 15 (right) © Barry Staver/People Magazine; p. 15 (left) © Gamma.

Cynthia Ellis
James Minor
Michael Murphy
David Omer
Rick Williams
Sandy Wilson

Cover Photography: © Michael Simpson/FPG

Illustration Credits: Cath Polito

ISBN: 0-8114-9222-2

Contents

Scope and Sequence

Book Title	Sight Words/Vocabulary	Phonics/Word Study
Introductory Book	<ul><li>Visual discrimination of letters/words</li><li>Recognition of letters of the alphabet</li><li>Sight words in context</li><li>Question words (*who, what, when, where, why*)</li><li>157 words total</li></ul>	<ul><li>Initial and final consonants</li><li>Short vowels and CVC word pattern</li><li>Long vowels and CVC + *e* word pattern</li></ul>
Book One	<ul><li>Introduces 107 sight words, function words, and number words</li><li>Reviews 143 words from the *Introductory Book*</li></ul>	<ul><li>Letter-sound associations reviewed for Consonants Short vowels and CVC word pattern Long vowels and CVC + *e* word pattern</li></ul>
Book Two	<ul><li>Sight word pages introduce 63 new words</li><li>Review word pages reinforce 143 words from the *Introductory Book* and 107 words from *Book 1*</li></ul>	<ul><li>Short vowels taught and reviewed through these word families: Short *a* in *-at, -an, -ad, -and* Short *e* in *-end, -ent, -et, -ed* Short *o* in *-op, -ot* Short *i* in *-in, -it* Short *u* in *-ut, -un*</li><li>Initial consonants reviewed and recycled</li></ul>
Book Three	<ul><li>Sight word pages introduce 63 new words</li><li>Review word pages reinforce 84 sight words from *Books 1–2*</li></ul>	<ul><li>Long vowels taught and reviewed through these word families: Long *a* in *-ake, -ay* Long *i* in *-ine, -ight* Long *o* in *-ope, -old* Long *e* in *-eed, -eat* Long *u* in *-une, -ute*</li><li>Short vowels reviewed through these word families: *-ag, -ell, -ip, -ig, -ug*</li><li>Initial consonant blends introduced in context: *st, sh, wh, pr, dr, str, th, cl, tr*</li></ul>

# of Program Strands

Language/Writing	Comprehension/Life Skills
• Writing letters of the alphabet • Writing words and sentences • Language experience stories • Journal writing	• Finding the main idea • Recalling facts and details
• Antonyms • Adding -s to form plurals • Adding -s, -ed, and -ing endings to verbs • Writing sentences • Language experience stories • Journal writing	• Predicting • Summarizing • Recalling facts and details • Finding the main idea
• Forming plurals with -s • Adding -s, -ed, and -ing to verbs • Forming contractions • Capitalizing sentences and proper names • Adding 's to form singular possessive of nouns • Doubling the final consonant to add -ed and -ing to verbs • Writing sentences • Journal writing	• **Comprehension skills:** predicting, summarizing, recalling facts and details, finding the main idea, inferring, sequencing events, drawing conclusions, determining cause and effect • **Life skills:** managing money, moving to find work, maintaining health, using leisure time, job safety, understanding self and others, selecting a satisfying job
• Compound words • Irregular plurals • Adding -er to nouns • End punctuation of sentences • Irregular verbs • Dropping final e to add -ed and -ing to verbs • Using quotation marks in dialog • Writing sentences • Journal writing	• **Comprehension skills:** predicting, summarizing, recalling facts and details, finding the main idea, inferring, sequencing events, drawing conclusions, determining cause and effect • **Life skills:** finding ways to increase income, rearing children, promoting health care, handling social relationships, learning about training programs, coping with job dissatisfaction, working together for change

Scope and Sequence

Book Title	Sight Words/Vocabulary	Phonics/Word Study

Book Four	• Sight word pages introduce 84 new words
	• Review word pages reinforce 84 sight words from *Books 2–3*
	• Life Skill pages introduce 28 new words
		• Consonant blends taught:
		  r blends: *br, cr, dr, fr, gr, pr, str, tr*
		  s blends: *sc, sk, sm, sn, sp, st, str, sw*
		  l blends: *bl, cl, fl, gl, pl, sl*
		• Consonant digraphs taught: *ch, sh, shr, th, wh*
		• Silent letters taught: *wr, kn, gu, gh*
		• Long vowels *i* and *e* spelled *-y* taught
		• Long and short vowels reviewed through these word families: *-ay, -ack, -ank, -ate, -ean, -ear, -eep, -eet, -ight, -in, -ine, -ink, -ing, -ock, -ub, -y*
		• Syllables defined
		• Vowel sound as schwa introduced

Book Five	• Sight word pages introduce 84 new words • Review word pages reinforce 84 sight words from *Books 3–4* • Life Skill pages introduce 30 new words	• Vowel digraphs taught through these word families: *-age, -aid, -ain, -ame, -ape, -ay, -ie, -ice, -ight, -ind, -ive, -ook, -ool, -oon, -ue, -ew, -all, -aw* • Diphthongs taught through these word families: *-oil, -oy, -own, -ound, -oup, -ow* • R-controlled vowels taught through these word families: *-ark, -art, -irl, -ork, -orn, and -urse* • Consonant blends and digraphs reviewed and recycled • Syllables and schwa reviewed

Book Six	• Definition pages introduce 70 new words
	• Vocabulary pages cover the following skills:
	  Multiple meanings Suffixes
	  Word stress Prefixes
	  Antonyms Analogies
	  Dictionary entries
	• Vocabulary, word study, and life skills pages introduce new words in context
		• Dividing words into syllables using VCV, VCCV, and consonant + *le* word patterns
		• Dictionary entries
		• Dictionary pronunciations
		• Dictionary accent marks

# of Program Strands

Language/Writing	Comprehension	Life Skills
• Irregular verbs • Prefixes *re-* and *un-* • Plurals with *-ies* • Suffixes *-ly, -ful, -ness, -y* • Abbreviations and titles • Days of the week and months of the year • Journal writing	• Predicting • Summarizing • Cause and effect • Inference • Stated and implied main idea • Sequence • Context • Drawing conclusions	• Writing a letter • Reading coupons • Reading a report card • Reading a prescription • Reading park rules • Coping with shyness • Reading a schedule
• Word building skills reviewed: forming plurals; adding *-s, -ed,* and *-ing;* adding prefixes and suffixes • Adding *-er* and *-est* to adjectives • Writing a friendly letter • Changing *y* to *i* to add *-es, -ed* • Forming plural possessive of nouns • Reflexive pronouns • Plurals with *-es* • Irregular verbs • Journal writing	• Predicting • Summarizing • Fact and opinion • Comparing and contrasting • Sequence • Inference • Making judgments • Drawing conclusions • Classifying	• Reading help wanted ads • Payment schedule • Reading a map • Telephone safety • Reading ads • Filling out a form • Reading a menu
• Using adjectives • Writing names and titles • Writing complete sentences • Recognizing fragments • Past tense of verbs • Pronouns • Recognizing run-ons • Journal writing	• Predicting • Summarizing • Recalling facts • Character traits • Main idea • Cause and effect • Inference • Sequence • Drawing conclusions • Writer's tone and purpose • Fact and opinion	• Finding library materials • Registering to vote • Writing a summary of qualifications • Completing a medical form • Filling out a credit application • Being a good listener • Reading abbreviations

DISCUSSION

Remember
Look at the picture. What work do you think this man does?

Predict
Look at the picture and the story title. What do you think the story is about?

Instructor's Notes: Read the discussion questions with students. Discuss the story title and the situation in the picture. Explain that this story is based on the life of a real person.

One Man, Many Jobs: Ben Nighthorse Campbell

Ben Nighthorse Campbell is a man with many jobs. Some of the time, he's working on his land. Some of the time he's in the city doing the job he was picked to do, taking action on problems people have. When he has time, he works on the job that he learned as a child.

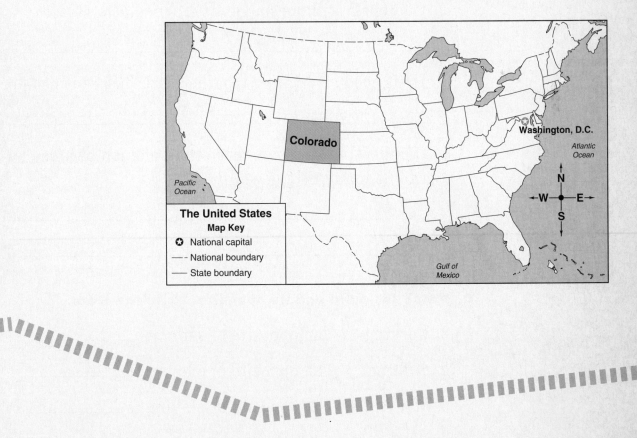

The United States
Map Key
- ✪ National capital
- – · – National boundary
- —— State boundary

Colorado

Washington, D.C.

Pacific Ocean

Atlantic Ocean

Gulf of Mexico

N W E S

Instructor's Notes: Read Campbell's full name and have students repeat it. Explain that Campbell is from the state of Colorado. Then have students read silently. Have them underline words they don't recognize. Review the underlined words. Discuss what is located in Washington, D.C.

Review Words

A. Check the words you know.

☐ 1. still   ☐ 2. because   ☐ 3. hold

☐ 4. many   ☐ 5. working   ☐ 6. people

☐ 7. together   ☐ 8. different   ☐ 9. does

☐ 10. action   ☐ 11. child   ☐ 12. more

B. Read and write the sentences. Circle the review words.

1. Ben Nighthorse Campbell takes action in many different ways.

   _____

2. Campbell still does a job he learned as a child.

   _____

3. He is good at working together with different people.

   _____

4. Campbell holds down more than one job because he can do many things well.

   _____

   _____

C. Match the word and its opposite. Write the word.

1. working   The opposite of <u>same</u> is _____.

2. different   The opposite of <u>one</u> is _____.

3. many   The opposite of <u>playing</u> is _____.

Instructor's Notes: Read each set of directions with students. For A, have students read the words aloud and then check known words. Have students practice any unknown words in a notebook or journal. For C, explain that words that are opposite are also called *antonyms*.

Sight Words

law
been
Native American
here

A. Read the words in color. Then read the sentence.

Laws have been helping Native Americans here in the U.S.

B. Underline the sight words in sentences 1–5.

1. Ben Nighthorse Campbell is a Native American.

2. He has been of help to people with problems.

3. Campbell works to make bills into laws.

4. Native Americans want action on these laws.

5. There have been problems about the water rights of different groups of people here in the U.S.

C. Write the word that completes each sentence.

Native Americans   laws   here   been

1. Campbell's home is _____ in the U.S.

2. He works on water rights for _____.

3. He has _____ a key player in taking action.

4. How does Campbell help make _____ ?

D. Read the sentences. Underline the sight words.

The land and water in the U.S. are different from when Native Americans owned the land. People came to the U.S. to make homes in this country and took a lot of the land. They have used up or hurt the water in some way. Campbell feels that people can work to make laws that fix these problems.

Instructor's Notes: Read each set of directions with students. For A, read each sight word aloud. Have students repeat. Discuss the use of the terms Native American and American Indian. Explain that Senator Campbell works to protect natural resources and public lands in Colorado.

Sight Words

elected
senator
horse
ranch

A. Read the words in color. Then read the sentences.

Campbell was <u>elected</u> <u>senator</u> in the fall of 1992.
Sometimes he has to put the work on his <u>horse</u> <u>ranch</u>
on hold.

B. Underline the sight words in sentences 1–3.

1. People elected Campbell because he is a man of action.

2. A senator is elected to help make laws.

3. Senator Campbell owns and runs a horse ranch
   as well.

C. Write the word that completes each sentence.

horses   senator   ranch   elected

1. Senators are _____ by the people.

2. Being a _____ is a big job.

3. One of Campbell's many loves is working on his

   _____ .

4. He works with quarter _____ on his ranch.

D. Read the sentences. Underline the sight words.

At his ranch, Senator Campbell can ride horses and
work with his ranch hands. He doesn't have the time
for his ranch that he used to, but he gets there when he
can. He gives his job as senator his all because he was
elected by the people.

Instructor's Notes: Read each set of directions with students. For A, read each sight word aloud. Have students repeat. Explain that Colorado is Campbell's home state and where his ranch is located. As a senator, he works in Washington, D.C. Have students review the map on page 7.

Sight Words

put
silver
jewelry
again

A. Read the words in color. Then read the sentence.

With all the work Campbell has to <u>put</u> in as a senator and a rancher, he will have to find time to make <u>silver</u> <u>jewelry</u> <u>again</u>.

B. Underline the sight words in sentences 1–4.

1. Campbell learned how to make jewelry when he was a child.

2. Campbell's teacher in jewelry making was his father.

3. He sometimes puts stones in his silver jewelry.

4. People who like his work come to him for jewelry again.

C. Write the word that completes each sentence.

> jewelry   silver   again   puts

1. You can see the time Campbell _____ into his work.

2. The _____ jewelry is sold in stores.

3. People look at it _____ and again.

4. Campbell likes to put horses on his _____ .

D. Read the sentences. Underline the sight words.

Will Campbell find time to make more silver jewelry? He says he won't give up doing work he likes this well. He works on the silver jewelry at night. That way he can go to his job as senator again in the daytime and still put in time on what he likes, making silver jewelry.

Instructor's Notes: Read each set of directions with students. Encourage students to practice writing sentences from Review Word and Sight Word pages in a notebook or journal.

11

Phonics: Syllables

A. Say the words aloud. Listen to the parts in each word. Some words have one part or <u>syllable</u>; some have two syllables.

One Syllable	Two Syllables	
ranch	because	be-cause
time	silver	sil-ver
job	again	a-gain
works	person	per-son
put	people	peo-ple
drive	ago	a-go

B. Say each word aloud. Listen to the number of syllables in each word. Write the word under the correct heading.

law
problem
more
rancher
safety
father
group
country
own
like

One Syllable	Two Syllables
1. _____	1. _____
2. _____	2. _____
3. _____	3. _____
4. _____	4. _____
5. _____	5. _____

C. Read the sentences. Draw one line under one-syllable words. Draw two lines under two-syllable words.

1. Ben Campbell holds down many jobs.

2. Campbell owns a horse ranch.

3. Sometimes he works with silver.

4. He puts in time working for people.

Instructor's Notes: Read each set of directions with students. Explain that each syllable always contains one vowel sound. Help students sound out syllables.

Phonics: Syllables and Schwa

A. Say the words aloud. Listen for the number of word parts you hear in each word. Each part is called a syllable. Each syllable has one vowel sound.

I Syllable	2 Syllables	3 Syllables
horse	own-er	fam-i-ly
been	man-y	sen-a-tor
hold	work-ing	jew-el-ry
life	Sen-ate	to-geth-er
things	quar-ter	e-lect-ed

B. Listen for how many syllables you hear in each word. Write the number.

wallet _____   different _____   someone _____

plan _____   learned _____   uniform _____

value _____   street _____   video _____

C. Listen for the vowel sound in the underlined syllables below. This vowel sound is called the schwa. Each of the vowels—a̲, e̲, i̲, o̲, or u̲—can stand for the schwa sound.

a	e	i	o	u
a̲-bout	sil-ver̲	fam-i̲-ly	lem-on̲	cac-tu̲s

D. Listen for the schwa sound in the words below. Write the letter that stands for the schwa sound.

again _____   doctor _____   parent _____

holiday _____   problem _____   person _____

Instructor's Notes: Read each set of directions with students. Help students sound out syllables in A and B. Explain that the schwa sound is shown in the dictionary by the symbol ə. Go over the examples for the schwa sound in C.

Language: Suffixes -ly and -y

friend + ly = friendly   health + y = healthy

A suffix is a word part added to the end of a word that changes the meaning of the word. The suffix –ly means "how something is done." The suffix –y means "full of" or "like." These suffixes are added to the words to describe people or things.

A. Add the suffix. Write the new word.

Add –ly	Add –y
1. different _____	1. need _____
2. love _____	2. hand _____
3. safe _____	3. hill _____
4. like _____	4. luck _____
5. night _____	5. might _____

B. Read the paragraph. Underline the words ending in –ly or –y.

Campbell does things differently. He holds down more than one job, and he works for needy causes. The people are lucky that they elected him senator. His friendly ways are likely to get him elected again.

C. Write the word that fits best in each sentence.

lovely   handy   nightly   hilly

1. Campbell works on his jewelry _____.

2. Isn't the silver jewelry _____?

3. Campbell is _____ at doing many things.

Instructor's Notes: Discuss the examples with students. Read each set of directions with students. For A, explain that suffixes add another syllable to each word. Have students read the new words formed.

BACK TO THE STORY

■■■■■■■■■■ **Remember**

What have you learned about Senator
Campbell so far?

■■■■■■■■■■ **Predict**

Look at the pictures. What do you think the
rest of the story will be about?

One Man, Many Jobs:
Ben Nighthorse Campbell

Native Americans have been working with silver for
some time. It takes time to learn to make jewelry well.
Silver can be bent or it can be cut with a saw. The person
working with silver can't take chances. Making silver
jewelry is fine hand work.

Instructor's Notes: Read the questions with students. Help students review and predict. Then have
students read the story silently.

15

Many jewelry makers cut lines into the silver. On a clip or pin, they may cut lines that stand for the family that makes the jewelry. Senator Campbell likes to put horses on his jewelry because of his Native American name, Ben Nighthorse, and his love for horses.

He sells a lot of his jewelry, but he gives some of it to groups of people who work for the same causes he does, helping Native Americans and the land. Sometimes people tell Campbell what they want him to put on the jewelry he makes for them. Both men and women like and buy his silver jewelry.

Senator Campbell has been willing to take all the time needed to do a job well. He learned to make jewelry at the age of 12. He earned his G.E.D. and went on to get a B.A. using money he earned as a truck driver. He met different people and went to different lands on his own. Campbell worked with Native Americans in prison to help them with the problems of coping with prison life. He wanted to help Native Americans and all the people of this country. He took action by running for senator and getting elected.

Campbell is a man who does many things well. He likes what he can do in his job as senator for people with problems. He feels he can use what he has learned from his own life in his job as senator. He likes the jewelry he makes with his own hands. He loves working with the horses on his ranch. Campbell's family helps him in his jobs when he isn't in the Senate. His wife helps him on the ranch, and his son helps him make jewelry. Making jewelry, running a ranch, and being a senator make up a good life for Ben Nighthorse Campbell.

Instructor's Notes: Explain to students that Campbell traveled to Japan and was on the 1964 U.S. Olympic judo team.

The time is right for a Native American senator. There are many different groups in our country today. All of them want to have a say in how the country is run. People want senators who will stand up for them and work to get the laws they need. That's why Ben Nighthorse Campbell ran for the Senate and why many women were elected in 1992. All groups have the right to elect someone to the Senate who will see that their needs are met.

Senators talk with the people who elected them to find out if they are doing a good job. Senator Campbell likes talking to people as well as working on his ranch and making silver jewelry. He will keep doing all three jobs because he feels a life of action is the life for him.

Comprehension

Think About It

1. Why did people elect Campbell to be senator?
2. What do you know about the work a senator does?
3. What other work does Campbell do?
4. Sum up what makes Campbell a man of action.

Write About It

How could you benefit from having more than one job? How could having more than one job create problems?

Instructor's Notes: Help students read and answer the questions. **Write About It** can be used as a writing or discussion assignment.

Tips for Finding Cause and Effect

When you ask, "**Why** did this happen?" you are looking for a **cause**.
When you ask, "**What happened**?" you are looking for an **effect**.

Example: He was elected senator because people like him.

    effect   cause

Use these tips to find the cause or the effect.

1. Look for cause words such as *the reason for*, *because*, *caused by*, *since*, and *why*.
2. Look for effect words such as *so* and *as a result*.

A. Read the sentence and find the cause. Circle the cause.

He puts horses on his jewelry

1. and works with horses on his ranch.
2. after he cuts the silver.
3. because of his name, Ben Nighthorse.

B. Read the sentence and find the effect. Circle the effect.

He wanted to help people with problems

1. so he ran for senator.
2. and wanted to be a senator.
3. by talking to them.

C. Read the sentence. Underline the cause. Circle the effect.

Since Campbell is a Native American, he took the name Ben Nighthorse.

Instructor's Notes: Discuss the tips with students. Then read the directions with students. Have students write sentences using cause and effect words in a notebook or journal.

Life Skill: Writing a Letter

letter
government
Congress
signature

A. Read the words in color. Then read the letter. Look at the five parts of the letter.

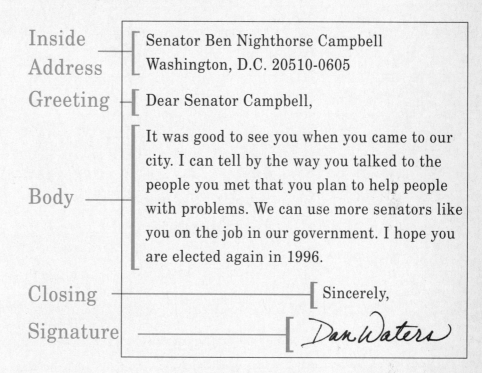

Inside
Address
: Senator Ben Nighthorse Campbell
Washington, D.C. 20510-0605

Greeting : Dear Senator Campbell,

Body : It was good to see you when you came to our city. I can tell by the way you talked to the people you met that you plan to help people with problems. We can use more senators like you on the job in our government. I hope you are elected again in 1996.

Closing : Sincerely,

Signature : *Dan Waters*

B. Match the parts of a letter to what each part tells you.

_____ 1. inside address   a. your name

_____ 2. closing   b. name and address of the person you're writing to

_____ 3. signature   c. saying good-bye

C. Write a letter to your senator or congressman. Find the information you need to write the letter from one of the following places.

- Government listings in the telephone book
- Local newspaper
- Voter registration office in your area

Instructor's Notes: Read the new words and each set of directions with students. Go over the parts of a letter and explain the *return address*. Help students find the information for C and assist them in writing a letter. Use the Unit I Review on page 104 to conclude the unit. Then assign *Reading for Today Workbook Four*, Unit I.

DISCUSSION

Remember

Look at the picture. Do you ever use coupons when you buy food?

Predict

Look at the picture and the story title. What do you think this story is about?

Instructor's Notes: Read the discussion questions with students. Discuss the story title and the situation in the picture.

Do You Need To Buy It?

Nan: Say, Sis, what do we have to eat? I don't want to pay to eat out when I can eat at home.

Kay: Look up there and see. I get things all the time. I take a lot of time at the store finding good buys.

Nan: Well . . . I see eight cans of nuts, some hot dog buns, and a lot of pop. But these foods don't go together well. What is going on?

Kay: When I go to the store, I shop with these! They help me use my money well.

Nan: You are right. And these can help a lot when they are for things we need. But you are buying things that we don't need. You have to look at what we have. I don't like paying for something that we don't need.

Kay: I see—you want me to buy the things you want to eat, right? Maybe you need to do the shopping, Sis. That will help you see the problems I have to cope with!

Instructor's Notes: Have students read silently. Have them underline words they don't recognize. Review the underlined words. Have students identify the speakers in the picture and their relationship to each other.

Review Words

A. Check the words you know.

- ☐ 1. baseball
- ☐ 2. game
- ☐ 3. thing
- ☐ 4. because
- ☐ 5. many
- ☐ 6. need
- ☐ 7. buyer
- ☐ 8. sell
- ☐ 9. seven
- ☐ 10. these
- ☐ 11. see
- ☐ 12. want

B. Read and write the sentences. Circle the review words.

1. Buyers like Kay want all the things they see.

   _____

2. Do they buy because they need all these things?

   _____

3. Kay doesn't need many of the things she buys.

   _____

4. Store owners can make money when they sell to buyers like Kay.

   _____

   _____

C. Read the clues. Choose a review word for the answer.

1. a game played with a bat and ball _____

2. one more than six _____

3. something a child likes to play _____

Instructor's Notes: Read each set of directions with students. For A, have students read the words aloud and then check known words. Have students practice any unknown words in a notebook or journal.

Sight Words

could
coupon
then
save

A. Read the words in color. Then read the sentence.

We could use coupons and then save money.

B. Underline the sight words in sentences 1–5.

1. I read the ads and then clip out the coupons.

2. Do I need to save all the coupons I see?

3. Could they help me save on something I need?

4. I could clip out the coupons I want to use.

5. Then I could use the coupons to get the things I need.

C. Write the word that completes each sentence.

save   then   coupons   could

1. You _____ give me some tips about using coupons when I shop.

2. Cutting out _____ can take a lot of time.

3. Save a lot of coupons and _____ go shopping.

4. You don't _____ money when you buy things that you don't need.

D. Read the sentences. Underline the sight words.

Nan and Kay want to save money when they shop. One way they could save money is to use coupons. Nan finds coupons in the store ads, and then Kay clips out the ones that could help them save. They save a lot of coupons and then buy the things they need.

Instructor's Notes: Read each set of directions with students. For A, read each sight word aloud. Have students repeat.

23

Sight Words

much
less
think
cost

A. Read the words in color. Then read the sentence.

How <u>much</u> <u>less</u> do you <u>think</u> meat will <u>cost</u> with a coupon?

B. Underline the sight words in sentences 1–4.

1. Many people could pay less using coupons, but they don't think about it.

2. The right way to use coupons is to think about what you are buying.

3. How much money does meat cost without the coupon?

4. Will meat cost more or less at a different store?

C. Write the word that completes each sentence.

much   less   cost   think

1. We use more coupons and pay _____ money.

2. I _____ the store will take our coupons.

3. How _____ meat do we need to buy?

4. Meat might _____ more at a different store.

D. Read the sentences. Underline the sight words.

Food costs more and more these days. I think we could save money by using coupons. But we have to think about some things when we shop. How much does food cost when we use coupons? Will the cost be less at a big store that has a lot of goods? How much trouble is it to get to that store?

Instructor's Notes: Read each set of directions with students. For A, read each sight word aloud. Have students repeat.

Sight Words

why
roommate
spend
too

A. Read the words in color. Then read the sentence.

<u>Why</u> does my <u>roommate</u> <u>spend</u> <u>too</u> much money?

B. Underline the sight words in sentences 1–5.

1. My roommate saves all the coupons she sees.

2. Then she spends money for things we don't need.

3. When we shop together, she doesn't buy too much.

4. Why can't she do that when I'm not with her?

5. I think my roommate could learn to stop buying things we don't need.

C. Write the word that completes each sentence.

too	roommate	Why	spend

1. _____ do you think people save coupons?

2. Things cost _____ much money today.

3. I think that my _____ needs help shopping.

4. Why _____ more when you can save with coupons?

D. Read the sentences. Underline the sight words.

My roommate has a problem when she goes shopping without me. She spends money on things we don't need because she thinks she saves money. Then we have too many things, but not what we need. Why do store ads and coupons make people want things they can't use? I'm going to help my roommate quit buying things we don't need.

Phonics: Consonant Blends with r

A. **Listen to the beginning sound in each word below.**
Underline the letters that stand for the r blend.

<u>br</u>	<u>cr</u>	<u>dr</u>	<u>fr</u>
brand	cream	drive	friend
brag	crop	drop	from

<u>gr</u>	<u>pr</u>	<u>tr</u>	<u>str</u>
group	problem	trouble	street
gray	prison	truck	strap

B. **Make other words with r blends. Read and write the words.**

–ay	–ip
gr + ay = _____	dr + ip = _____
fr + ay = _____	gr + ip = _____
tr + ay = _____	str + ip = _____
str + ay = _____	tr + ip = _____

C. **Choose the right word for each sentence below.**

1. (bag, brag) Kay likes to _____ about the money she saves.

2. (trip, tip) Kay and I went on a big shopping _____ .

3. (brand, band) She used a coupon to buy a good _____ of hot dogs.

4. (ray, tray) We had a big _____ full of hot dogs to eat.

Instructor's Notes: Read each set of directions with students. For A, have students read the words aloud. Explain that the two consonant letters (three for *str*) blend together for the sound at the beginning of each word, but that students can still hear the consonant sound of each letter.

Phonics: –y and –ink

why
by
my

A. Read the words in color. Write other –y words.

cr + y = _____

dr + y = _____

fr + y = _____

tr + y = _____

B. Write a –y word to finish each sentence.

1. I think _____ roommate uses too many coupons when she shops.

2. Kay said she will _____ not to buy food we don't need.

3. _____ did she buy all these hot dogs?

think
pink
rink
sink

C. Read the words in color. Write other –ink words.

w + ink = _____

br + ink = _____

dr + ink = _____

D. Write an –ink word to finish each sentence.

1. When I was a child, I liked to _____ pop.

2. My sister got 12 cans for us to _____ .

3. I don't _____ we needed that much pop.

Instructor's Notes: Explain to students that the –y stands for the long *i* sound in the known sight word *why* and many other one-syllable words ending in –y. Then show students the –ink word pattern in the known sight word *think*. The –ink words have the short *i* sound. Read each set of directions with students.

Language: Irregular Verbs

save—saved   think—thought

Add –ed to some verbs to show the past. For other words, change the spelling to show the past.

Examples: I think of my sister. (I am doing it <u>now</u>.)

I thought of my sister a lot. (I did it in the <u>past</u>.)

A. Read this list of verbs.

Present	Past	Present	Past
sell	sold	are	were
begin	began	find	found
give	gave	take	took
buy	bought	pay	paid
teach	taught	spend	spent

B. Read the paragraph. Underline the irregular verbs.

I gave some coupons to my roommate, and she took them to the store. Kay thought all the coupons were good, and she bought a lot of things. Then she found out the coupons were good in May, but not in June. I hope this taught Kay to read coupons well.

C. Complete each sentence by choosing the verb that tells about the past.

1. Someone at the store _____ my roommate a radio.
   sell sold

2. The trouble was that Kay _____ too much for it.
   pay paid

Instructor's Notes: Discuss the examples with students. Explain that irregular verbs show past tense by changing spelling instead of adding –d or –ed. Read each set of directions with students.

BACK TO THE STORY

Remember
What has happened in the story so far?

Predict
Look at the picture. What do you think the women are doing? What do you think will happen in the rest of the story?

Do You Need to Buy It?

Kay: Nan, look at all these coupons! We could save big money this way. This is a good one . . . we buy seven cans of dog food and send in this coupon. Then they send us seven more cans!

Nan: That could be a good saving for us, Kay, but we don't have a dog!

Instructor's Notes: Read the questions with students. Help students review and predict. Have students read the story silently or ask students if they want to take parts in reading the story aloud.

29

Kay: OK . . . but this coupon is right for us. We can save ten cents on figs at the health food store. They cost much more at the store down the street.

Nan: Figs? Who likes figs in this home? What a roommate you are. You spend money on things we don't need because you think you are getting a good buy. It ends up costing us more money, not less money!

Kay: OK, Nan, I see why you don't want me to buy things we don't need. Good buyers don't use all the coupons they see. But I may need help from you, Sis.

Nan: Then give me these ads! I'll find some coupons we can use. Say! We could win tickets to a baseball game in May with this coupon. All we need to do is cut out the coupons from the hot dogs we buy and send them in. What do you think?

Kay: You don't have to sell me on baseball. I love ball games . . . and hot dogs, too.

Nan: We'll have to buy many, many hot dogs, Kay, because we need 50 coupons to win the tickets.

[Many days go by . . .]

Kay: I don't think I like these hot dogs, Nan. Why don't we go out to eat?

Nan: We bought them to win the tickets for the baseball game. And we can't go out to eat because I spent all our food money on hot dogs.

Kay: But Nan, how much can a person spend on hot dogs? And how many hot dogs can we eat without getting sick? Well, you do think we'll win, don't you?

Nan: We'll win something because we did what the coupon said. What more could we do?

[More days go by . . .]

Kay: Nan, look what came for us! It's from the coupon people, and I bet it's our tickets to the baseball game. I can tell this is our lucky day.

Nan: No! It can't be! Read this!

Kay: What is it, Nan? Did we lose?

Nan: We didn't lose, but we didn't win the baseball tickets. We're getting more hot dogs! They are on the way to us.

Kay: I think I'm going to be sick. I'm sick of seeing hot dogs and coupons. This has taught me the right way to use coupons. I found out that trying to save money can sometimes cost me money. I have to think about what I'm buying.

Comprehension

Think About It

1. Why did Kay and Nan have to eat so many hot dogs?
2. What did Kay and Nan win?
3. What did Kay learn about coupons?
4. Sum up what happened in the story.

Write About It

Do you think coupons are useful? Explain why or why not.

Instructor's Notes: Help students read and answer the questions. **Write About It** can be used as a writing or discussion assignment.

Comprehension: Inference

> **Tips for Making Inferences**
>
> An **inference** is an idea you get by putting facts together.
> **Example:** Jay saves his money. (Fact)
> Then he buys tickets for baseball games. (Fact)
> Jay likes baseball. (Inference)
>
> **Use these tips to make an inference.**
> 1. Read the story.
> 2. List the facts that are stated.
> 3. Put the facts together to come up with your inference.

A. Read this paragraph.

Matt looked at the coupons. They were for tea bags. Matt gave the coupons to Kay. She used them when she went to the store.

B. List the facts.

Fact 1 _____

Fact 2 _____

Fact 3 _____

Fact 4 _____

C. Circle the inference you can make from the facts.

1. Matt saves coupons.

2. The coupons were no good.

3. Kay likes tea.

Instructor's Notes: Discuss the tips with students. Then read the directions together.

Life Skill: Reading Coupons

A. Read the words in color. Then read the coupons below.

longer
ounces (oz.)
word
expiration

1.

MANUFACTURER'S COUPON   NO EXPIRATION DATE

50¢

New! **Bright** LAUNDRY DETERGENT

171 OZ.

SAVE 50¢
WHEN YOU BUY
ONE FAMILY SIZE (171 oz.)
OR THREE REGULAR SIZE (20 oz.)

9 780811 488754

50¢

2.

15¢   **SAVE 15¢**   15¢

on a 16-oz. package of
Oscar Buyer Hot Dogs

To the store owner:
Oscar Buyer Foods will give you the
value of this coupon and 7¢ for handling.
Customer will pay sales tax. This coupon
is good only on Oscar Buyer Hot Dogs.

HOT DOGS
OSCAR BUYER
16 oz.

15¢   MANUFACTURER'S COUPON EXPIRES: 8/8/95   15¢

B. Read the questions and write the answers.

1. One of the coupons is good for a longer time. Is it

   coupon 1 or coupon 2?_____

2. What word does oz. stand for in both coupons?

   _____

3. How much money can you save when you use

   coupon 1? _____   coupon 2? _____

Instructor's Notes: Read the new words and each set of directions with students. Read and discuss the coupons with students. Use the Unit 2 Review on page 105 to conclude the unit. Then assign *Reading for Today Workbook Four*, Unit 2.

DISCUSSION

Remember

Look at the picture. What feelings do you see in the people's faces?

Predict

Read the title. What is your answer to the question? What do you think this story is about?

Instructor's Notes: Read the discussion questions with students. Discuss the story title and the situation in the picture.

Who Needs To Read?

Mr. Sanders is a man who has not learned to read. He has learned to get by in life. Someday he wants to take the time to have someone teach him to read. Something he wants more than that is for his son, Jay, to learn to read. He wants Jay's life to be different from his.

Jay has a problem with reading, too, but his family had not talked much about it. Then one night Jay told his dad that the teacher wanted to see his parents. It was time for the family to look into this problem.

When they sat at the table together that night, no one talked much. Jay looked down at his food without eating. The time to talk had come, but no one knew how to begin. When a father hasn't learned to read, how can he help his son learn?

Instructor's Notes: Have students read silently. Have them underline words they don't recognize. Review the underlined words. Point out the title *Mr.* that is part of the name *Mr. Sanders.*

Review Words

A. Check the words you know.

☐ 1. upset   ☐ 2. teach   ☐ 3. gave

☐ 4. together   ☐ 5. learn   ☐ 6. said

☐ 7. someone   ☐ 8. take   ☐ 9. down

☐ 10. teacher   ☐ 11. into   ☐ 12. who

B. Read and write the sentences. Circle the review words.

1. Will Jay be upset because I can't teach him to read?

   _____

2. I gave him help with baseball, but who will be his reading teacher?

   _____

   _____

3. When Jay takes time with his work, he does not get into trouble.

   _____

   _____

4. We'll all work together to help Jay learn to read.

   _____

C. Match each review word and its meaning.

_____ 1. down   a. a person

_____ 2. said   b. not up

_____ 3. someone   c. talked

Sight Words

mean

must

always

school

A. Read the words in color. Then read the sentence.

Does this <u>mean</u> that Jay <u>must</u> <u>always</u> have trouble in <u>school</u>?

B. Underline the sight words in sentences 1–5.

1. Mr. Sanders always wanted to go to school.

2. Going to school means you have a chance to learn.

3. Schools are not always for children.

4. A teacher must spend a lot of time helping people learn.

5. Does our teacher mean that we must always do well?

C. Write the word that completes each sentence.

must   always   mean   school

1. People don't have to go to _____ to learn.

2. Having a good teacher _____ helps you learn.

3. I _____ learn to read to help Jay.

4. Learning to read will _____ a chance for a good job.

D. Read the sentences. Underline the sight words.

Some parents think schools must always teach children to read. But children must get help at home with the things they learn at school. What does this mean for parents who can't read well? Sometimes these parents must get help, too.

Instructor's Notes: Read each set of directions with students. For A, read each sight word aloud. Have students repeat.

Sight Words

where

meet

soon

after

A. Read the words in color. Then read the sentence.

Tell me <u>where</u> we can <u>meet</u> <u>soon</u> <u>after</u> school.

B. Underline the sight words in sentences 1–5.

1. Mr. Sanders must meet his son's teacher soon.

2. Jay told his father where to find the teacher.

3. Mrs. Keating said she will meet Mr. Sanders.

4. Soon he will talk to her about Jay's problem.

5. After this talk, Mr. Sanders will help Jay.

C. Write the word that completes each sentence.

after   soon   Where   meet

1. Parents can see teachers _____ school.

2. Many teachers save this time of the day to _____ with parents.

3. Teachers don't go home _____ after the children.

4. _____ can Mr. Sanders find Jay's teacher?

D. Read the sentences. Underline the sight words.

Parents may have problems to work out when they meet with a teacher. They must find out where the school is. Sometimes both the child and parents must find a time to meet together with the teacher. Parents might need to be at home soon after work. But, when parents and teachers find time for these meetings, they can work out ways to help a child.

 Instructor's Notes: Read each set of directions with students. For A, read each sight word aloud. Have students repeat. Point out the title *Mrs.* that is part of the name *Mrs. Keating*.

Sight Words

or
grade
report
card

A. Read the words in color. Then read the sentence.

Did Jay get a good <u>or</u> bad <u>grade</u> on his <u>report</u> <u>card</u>?

B. Underline the sight words in sentences 1–5.

1. In school you may have to give a report.

2. Will you get a good or bad grade?

3. A report that makes the reader think will get a good grade.

4. Children don't get good grades on report cards because they are lucky.

5. Good grades mean the child did good work.

C. Write the word that completes each sentence.

card   or   report   grade

1. The teacher will like Jay's _____ .

2. He will get a good _____ from the teacher.

3. Did Jay's parents see his report _____ ?

4. Were they glad _____ upset about his grades?

D. Read the sentences. Underline the sight words.

What does a good grade on a report card mean?
It means the child did a lot of work to get the grade.
Some children have trouble giving a report. A parent
can help by talking with the child about what to say in
the report, or they can spend time reading it together.
Soon the child will get good grades on report cards.

Instructor's Notes: Read each set of directions with students. Continue journal writing.

Phonics: Consonant Blends with s

A. Listen to the beginning sound in each word below. Underline the letters that stand for the s blend.

sc	sk	sl	sm
scan	skin	slip	smoke
scold	sky	sled	smell

sn	sp	st	sw
snip	spend	stand	swim
snake	spell	store	sway

B. Make other words with s blends. Read and write the words.

−ay	−y
sl + ay = _____	sk + y = _____
st + ay = _____	sl + y = _____
sw + ay = _____	sp + y = _____

C. Choose the right word for each sentence below.

1. (sell, spell) Jay must learn to _____ and read well.

2. (say, stay) He will _____ after school to get help from his teacher.

3. (slip, sip) Jay won't let his grade _____ from a *D* to an *F* again.

4. (spend, send) Mr. Sanders wants to _____ time learning to read, too.

5. (sand, stand) Jay's parents will _____ by him and help him in school.

Instructor's Notes: Read each set of directions with students. For A, have students read the words aloud. Explain that the two consonant letters blend together for the sound at the beginning of each word, but that students can still hear the consonant sound of each letter.

Phonics: –eet and –ean

–eet
meet
beet
feet
street

A. Read the words in color. Write other –eet words.

gr + eet = _____

sl + eet = _____

sw + eet = _____

B. Write an –eet word to finish each sentence.

1. Mr. and Mrs. Sanders will go to Jay's school to

   _____ his teacher.

2. His teacher is a _____ person who loves children.

3. She will _____ Mr. Sanders with a handshake.

–ean
mean
bean
clean
lean

C. Read the words in color. Write other –ean words.

D + ean = _____

J + ean = _____

w + ean = _____

D. Write an –ean word to finish each sentence.

1. Jay's teacher is Mrs. _____ Keating.

2. She isn't a _____ teacher, but she makes Jay do his own work.

3. When Jay learns to read, he won't have to _____ on his friends for help.

Instructor's Notes: Show students the –eet word pattern in the known sight word *meet*. Then show students the –ean word pattern in the known sight word *mean*. Explain that –ee and –ea both spell the long e sound. Read each set of directions with students.

Language: Prefixes re– and un–

re + do = redo   un + do = undo

> A prefix is a word part added to the front of a word. The prefix gives the word a new meaning. The prefix re– means "to do again." The prefix un– means "not."

A. Add the prefix and write each new word.

Add re–		Add un–	
1. read	_____	1. lucky	_____
2. mind	_____	2. sold	_____
3. pay	_____	3. clear	_____
4. run	_____	4. loved	_____

B. Read the paragraph. Underline the words with prefixes.

Jay thinks he is unlucky to have a teacher who makes him work a lot. But someday he will want to repay her for her help. The teacher tells Jay that he must reread things many times. She makes him redo work that has mistakes in it.

C. Write the word that completes each sentence.

undo   remind   unclear   unloved

1. Sometimes what Jay reads is _____.

2. I'll _____ my son to do his homework.

3. Jay will _____ all the teacher's work if he does not read at home.

4. Children who get bad grades may feel _____.

Instructor's Notes: Discuss the examples with students. Read each set of directions with students. For A, have the students read the new words. Explain that prefixes add another syllable to each word.

BACK TO THE STORY

Remember
What has happened in the story so far?

Predict
Look at the picture. What do you think the family is talking about? What do you think will happen in the rest of the story?

Who Needs To Read?

 They sat at the table together that night, but the Sanders family wasn't talking at all. Mr. Sanders didn't look at his son Jay. Jay looked down at his food without eating.

"Well, Jay, it looks like we've got trouble," his father said in a sad way. "How could you get this grade on a report card? It says you can't read. The teacher gave you an *F* in reading and spelling."

Instructor's Notes: Read the questions with students. Help students review and predict. Then have students read the story silently. Explain to students that this story takes place at the Sanders' home and at Jay's school.

"What can I say? I'm unlucky in school," Jay said. "Or maybe the teacher gave me a bad grade because she doesn't like me." Then Jay looked up at his father. "Dad, why must I learn to read? After all, you can't read, and you always get by OK."

Mr. Sanders could not say what he was feeling. All he could think about was how much he had always wanted to learn to read. When he was a child, he got a job and quit school. Then he was a family man. After that, he had no time for school.

"I can't tell you how much I want to read," he said. "A person who can't read is helpless at times. When I need to read something, I always have to get help from someone. You must learn to read, Jay."

"Well, my teacher wants to meet with you and Mother about the grades on my report card," Jay said.

A meeting with the teacher reminded Mr. Sanders of his own school days. He had had many problems in his life then. To this day, talking about teachers, grades, and school still gave him trouble. But he wanted to help his son.

"I can go see her, but Mother needs to stay home with you," he said. "Where can I find the teacher?"

"She will be at the school tonight after seven," Jay said. "You can meet her in Room 10."

● ● ●

Mr. Sanders walked into Room 10 at a quarter after seven. A sweet-looking woman sat at the table. She looked up.

"I'm Mr. Sanders, Jay's father," he said. "I came about Jay's report card."

"Yes, Mr. Sanders. I was hoping you could come," the teacher greeted him. "I'm Jean Keating. Jay is having a lot of trouble in reading and spelling."

"Well, why don't you teach him to read?" Mr. Sanders said. "Isn't that a teacher's job?"

"Yes, but I must teach many children. Jay needs more help. He needs me at school and you at home."

Mr. Sanders looked down. He didn't want to tell her, but he must. "Mrs. Keating, I can't read. That is why I don't help Jay more. I always wanted to learn, but I don't know where to get help."

"There is a way you can help Jay. We work on reading here at the school two nights a week. Some of the people who come are parents like you. You'll find that you can learn what you want in less time than you think."

"I need to do this for my son and for me. We can learn together. I'll have to work to keep up with Jay!"

Mrs. Keating laughed with Mr. Sanders. "Well, you can always get an *A* in being a good father."

Comprehension

Think About It

1. Why didn't Mr. Sanders learn to read long ago?
2. Why does he want to learn now?
3. What does Jean Keating suggest that Mr. Sanders do?
4. Sum up what happened in the story.

Write About It

What's hard about learning to read? What's fun about it?

Instructor's Notes: Help students read and answer the questions. **Write About It** can be used as a writing or discussion assignment. Discuss the kind of class Mr. Sanders will probably be attending at his son's school and other literacy programs for adults.

Comprehension: Stated Main Idea

Tips for Finding the Stated Main Idea

The **main idea** is the point the writer is making.
Use these tips to find the main idea.

1. Read the whole paragraph or story.
2. Decide what the paragraph or story is about.
3. Check the first part of the paragraph. Often, the main idea is stated in the paragraph.

A. Underline the words that complete each sentence.

1. Jay isn't learning to read well because
   a. he is unlucky.
   b. he thinks he can get by without reading.
   c. his teacher is mean.

2. Jay's teacher can't spend more time with Jay because
   a. Jay has to work after school.
   b. she does not like him.
   c. she has many children to work with.

3. Mrs. Keating thinks that
   a. Jay's father is mean to Jay.
   b. Jay's father can help Jay.
   c. Jay's father needs a good job.

B. Pick the best choice for a new story title.

_____ Parents Are Teachers, Too

_____ Learning the Right Words

_____ Children and Homework

Instructor's Notes: Discuss the tips with students. Then read the directions together. Explain that a story title often gives the reader the main idea of the story.

Life Skill: Reading a Report Card

A. Read the words in color. Then read the report card below.

best

worst

name

math

Student: Jay Sanders	Grade: 3	School Name:
Teacher: Jean Keating		

SUBJECT AREAS				
	Reporting Periods			
	1	2	3	4
READING	B	C	C–	F
LANGUAGE	B	B	C	C
SPELLING	B	C	C–	F
MATHEMATICS	B	A	A–	A

PERSONAL DEVELOPMENT				
E - Excellent S - Satisfactory I - Improvement Needed U - Unsatisfactory				
	Reporting Periods			
	1	2	3	4
Follows directions	S	I	I	I
Completes assignments/homework	S	I	U	U
Turns work in on time	I	U	U	U

B. Read the questions and write the answers.

1. What did Jay make his best grade in?

   _____

2. What was Jay's worst grade? What was it in?

   _____

   _____

3. Does Jay do his work on time in reading and spelling? How do you know?

   _____

   _____

Instructor's Notes: Read the new words and each set of directions with students. Read and discuss the report card. Help students answer the questions. Use the Unit 3 Review on page 106 to conclude the unit. Then assign *Reading for Today Workbook Four*, Unit 3.

47

DISCUSSION

Remember

Look at the picture. How would you feel if there was a new child coming into your family?

Predict

Look at the picture and the story title. What do you think this story is about?

Instructor's Notes: Read the discussion questions with students. Discuss the story title and the situation in the picture.

A Family Man

What a lucky day this is for me! It's more like a holiday than a workday. Today Maria told me that I'm going to be a father! When she told me, I gave her a big hug. We wanted to both laugh and cry.

I must tell my family and friends. My parents will want to buy lots of things for the child. I bet they'll try to spend too much money. After the child comes, Maria's parents will drive up from the city to help out. Her best friend from down the street will go with her to the clinic.

We must think of a name for our child. Maria wants to name the child after her mother. I want a son to be named after my best friend. It's good that we have some time to think about a name.

I have a lot to learn about being a father, but my own father taught me a lot about being a loving parent. Maria will need my help with the heavy work at home. I'll take her to see the doctor, and I'll buy the right foods for her to eat. She must be in good health when the child comes. We're both smokers, but we'll quit for the child's sake. I'll do what I can to give this child a good life. I have big hopes for this family.

Instructor's Notes: Introduce the proper name *Maria*. Help students pronounce the name. Have students read silently. Have them underline words they don't recognize. Review the underlined words. Have students identify the speaker.

Review Words

A. Check the words you know.

☐ 1. child ☐ 2. come ☐ 3. clinic

☐ 4. doctor ☐ 5. hope ☐ 6. smoker

☐ 7. drive ☐ 8. hug ☐ 9. parents

☐ 10. heavy ☐ 11. up ☐ 12. street

B. Read and write the sentences. Circle the review words.

1. I gave Maria a hug when I learned about our child.

   _____

   _____

2. The doctor at the clinic said our child will come in June.

   _____

   _____

3. I'm a heavy smoker, but I hope to quit soon for our child's sake.

   _____

   _____

C. Choose review words to complete the puzzle.

Down
1. not down
2. a trip in a car
3. a road

Across
4. mother and father

Instructor's Notes: Read each set of directions with students. For A, have students read the words aloud and then check known words. Have students practice any unknown words in a notebook or journal. Explain to students that most crossword puzzles list words down, or *vertically*, and across, or *horizontally*.

Sight Words

as
responsible
wife
baby

A. Read the words in color. Then read the sentence.

As responsible parents, my wife and I will both look after our baby.

B. Underline the sight words in sentences 1–5.

1. My wife Maria is doing what the doctor told her.

2. We're learning how to be responsible parents.

3. My wife stopped smoking because it isn't good for the baby.

4. As a mother-to-be, she must think of her health.

5. Responsible parents always try to make a good life for children.

C. Write the word that completes each sentence.

wife   as   responsible   baby

1. My _____ and I will soon be parents.

2. Having a _____ means a lot to us.

3. We want to be _____ parents.

4. We'll try to spend ____ much time ____ we can with our child.

D. Read the sentences. Underline the sight words.

After my wife found out she was going to have a baby, we both stopped smoking. We're responsible for our baby's health. As our child gets big, we'll feel responsible for the child's schooling as well.

Instructor's Notes: Read each set of directions with students. For A, read each sight word aloud. Have students repeat. Explain that *mother-to-be* is another kind of compound word.

Sight Words

before
new
know
small

A. Read the words in color. Then read the sentence.

Before I'm a new father, I must know some things about small children.

B. Underline the sight words in sentences 1–5.

1. Before you know it, we'll have a new baby.

2. Do you think the baby will know that I'm a new father?

3. To be a good father, I must learn many new things.

4. I need to know how to carry a small child.

5. What do new parents feed a small baby?

C. Write the word that completes each sentence.

Small   know   new   Before

1. _____ our baby comes, I need to learn how to be a good father.

2. Is there a school for _____ parents?

3. We need to _____ a lot of things.

4. _____ children need lots of help.

D. Read the sentences. Underline the sight words.

We have a lot to think about before the baby comes. My wife and I will be responsible for a new life. Does a small child cry all night? Will I need to spend more time at home than I did before? We know our lives are going to be different, but we feel good about a new baby in our family.

Instructor's Notes: Read each set of directions with students. For A, read each sight word aloud. Have students repeat. Go over with students the differences between *new* and *knew* and then *know* and *no*.

Sight Words

pregnant
tired
rock
late

A. Read the words in color. Then read the sentences.

A <u>pregnant</u> woman may feel <u>tired</u> at times.
We will <u>rock</u> our baby <u>late</u> into the night.

B. Underline the sight words in sentences 1–4.

1. Maria's best friend Jan is pregnant, too.

2. Jan tells Maria that all pregnant women don't feel tired.

3. She rocks the baby to stop it from crying.

4. Jan says that new parents may feel tired from getting up late at night to feed the baby.

C. Write the word that completes each sentence.

tired   rock   late   pregnant

1. Get to the clinic before it's too _____ !

2. Dad used to _____ me when I was small.

3. Can a new father and mother get _____ ?

4. A group of _____ women meets at the clinic.

D. Read the sentences. Underline the sight words.

Maria was feeling tired, and she went to see the doctor. That was when she found out she is pregnant. I came home late that night, but she was up to tell me the good news. As soon as the baby comes, I want to spend time rocking our baby.

Instructor's Notes: Read each set with directions with students. Review contractions used on Sight Word pages. Continue journal writing. Review the uses of the period, the question mark, and the exclamation mark in writing sentences.

53

Phonics: Consonant Blends with l

A. Listen to the beginning sound in each word below. Underline the letters that stand for the l blend.

bl	cl	fl
blend	clinic	fly
blink	clan	flag

gl	pl	sl
glad	player	sly
gland	plan	sleet

B. Make other words with l blends. Read and write the words.

	−ink		−ight
bl + ink = _____		bl + ight = _____
cl + ink = _____		fl + ight = _____
pl + ink = _____		pl + ight = _____
sl + ink = _____		sl + ight = _____

C. Choose the right word for each sentence below.

1. (pan, plan) We need to _____ a name for the baby.

2. (plight, light) Staying up all night to rock the baby is the _____ of new parents.

3. (lad, glad) We're _____ that we'll have the chance to be good parents.

Instructor's Notes: Read each set of directions with students. For A, have students read the words aloud. Explain that the two consonant letters blend together for the sound at the beginning of each word, but that students can still hear the consonant sound of each letter.

Phonics: -ock and -ate

-ock
rock
lock
mock
sock

A. Read the words in color. Write other –ock words.

bl + ock = _____

cl + ock = _____

sm + ock = _____

B. Write an –ock word to finish each sentence.

1. Carlos plans to _____ the baby at night.

2. Maria got a big _____ to fit her.

3. Carlos looks at the _____ . Is it time to go to the clinic?

4. Our baby will play with the _____ we made.

-ate
late
date
gate
rate

C. Read the words in color. Write other –ate words.

pl + ate = _____

sk + ate = _____

st + ate = _____

D. Make an –ate word to finish each sentence.

1. I hope that our baby won't wake up _____ at night.

2. We have a _____ to see the doctor today.

3. The baby won't eat from a _____ for some time.

4. We can get a good _____ when we buy baby food.

Instructor's Notes: Explain that the *o* stands for the short vowel sound and the *ck* stands for one sound (*k*) in the known sight word *rock*. For the *–ate* words, explain that the *a* stands for the long vowel sound in the *a* + consonant + *e* pattern in the known sight word *late*. Read each set of directions with students.

Language: Plurals with –ies

baby + ies = babies   city + ies = cities

We add s to some words to mean more than one. If a word ends in a consonant plus y, we usually change the y to i and add –es to mean more than one.

A. Read the words and write the word that means more than one.

One	More Than One	
1. family	families	_____
2. cry	cries	_____
3. city	cities	_____
4. try	tries	_____
5. country	countries	_____

B. Read the paragraph. Underline the words that end in –ies.

Maria's parents and mine were from different countries. Then they came to this country, but they were in different cities. Our families did not meet before our wedding.

C. Write the word that completes each sentence.

cries   babies   countries   families

1. Our _____ will be glad about the baby.

2. We won't mind when the baby's _____ wake us.

3. Someday we want to have more _____ .

4. Many _____ have laws that help children.

Instructor's Notes: Discuss the examples with students. Explain that many words ending in y change the y to i and then add –es to form the plural. Read each set of directions with students.

BACK TO THE STORY

▪▪▪▪▪▪▪▪▪▪ **Remember**

What has happened in the story so far?

▪▪▪▪▪▪▪▪▪▪ **Predict**

Look at the picture. What do you think will happen in the rest of the story?

A Family Man

Maria: Carlos, before the end of the day, we'll be new parents. I can't help thinking about the day we found out I was pregnant.

Carlos: We were both glad, and our families were, too. How are you feeling? Do you want me to call the clinic and tell the doctor we'll be right there?

Maria: No, it's not time yet. You know, Carlos, we have not thought of a name for the baby. We'll need to have a name soon.

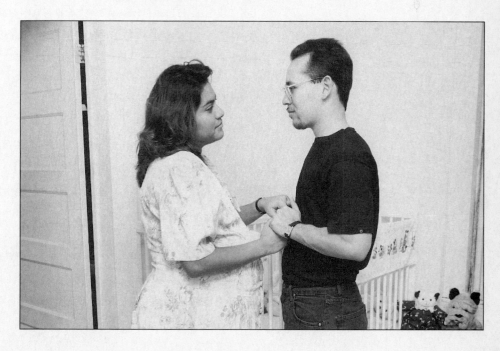

Instructor's Notes: Read the questions with students. Help students review and predict. Explain that *Carlos* is the name of Maria's husband in the story. Have students read the story silently or ask students if they want to take parts in reading the story aloud.

Carlos: I know . . . but I can't think of the right one. All I can think of is you. I hope that you don't have problems when the baby comes.

Maria: The doctor says the baby and I are both fine. I did as I was told at the clinic. I walked up and down our street two times a day. I didn't carry heavy things or get too tired. And I did not drive the car on big trips. The chances are good that I'll have no trouble when the baby comes.

Carlos: The doctor says it's a good thing that we stopped smoking when we learned that you are pregnant. When parents are smokers, small children in the home can get sick. As responsible parents, we had to quit.

Maria, I have big plans for this child. I've stocked our home with baby food and lots of small playthings. My brother lent us a baby bed. The baby will be in our room, with a rocker for us to sit in when we rock the baby. I hope we can be responsible parents, like our parents were for us.

Maria: I know that we can be, Carlos, but having a small child won't be all fun. Babies cry at all times of the day and night, and they have to be fed on time. New mothers and fathers feel tired a lot. Yes, this is going to be a new way of life for us.

Carlos: I'm lucky to have a wife who knows a lot about having a family. When you were a child, you had small brothers and sisters at home. That will help us both.

Maria: You know, there will be many times when our baby will need our help. We'll have to teach our child right from wrong. Children need help from parents to do well in school. And they need lots of hugs!

Carlos: It's a lot of work to be a responsible parent, but it will be fun, too. It will feel good to see our child learn to walk and talk. When our baby wakes up late at night, I'll be there to help you rock the baby. I hope this child gets here soon.

Maria: Carlos . . . I think you are going to get what you want. You must drive me to the clinic . . .

Carlos: Doctor! My wife is about to have the baby. We'll meet you at the clinic. Don't be late!

Comprehension

Think About It

1. Are Carlos and Maria glad about the baby? How do you know?
2. How will their lives change when the baby comes?
3. How will both parents help with the baby?
4. Sum up what happened in the story.

Write About It

How do the lives of a family change when a baby is born? Explain if the changes or good or bad, or both.

Instructor's Notes: Help students read and answer the questions. **Write About It** can be used as a writing or discussion assignment.

59

> **Tips for Finding an Implied Main Idea**
>
> A **main idea** is the main point the writer is making. If the main idea is not stated, we say it is **implied**. Then it's up to you, the reader, to find it.
>
> **Use these tips to find an implied main idea.**
> 1. Read the whole paragraph or story.
> 2. Decide what one main point all the sentences add up to. This is your clue to the implied main idea.

A. Read this paragraph.

Carlos and Maria want to be good parents. They learned from their own parents how to be responsible and loving. When the baby gets here, Carlos and Maria will both help tend the child.

B. Pick the best implied main idea. Circle it.

1. Carlos and Maria will be responsible parents.

2. Carlos and Maria will get their parents to tend the baby.

3. The baby will have a lot of fun.

C. Pick the best choice for a new story title.

_____ How To Pick a Good Doctor

_____ Maria and Carlos

_____ Responsible Parents

Life Skill: Reading a Prescription

A. Read the words in color. Then read the label below.

tablets
should
daily
bottle

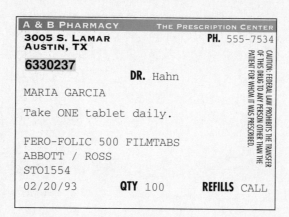

```
A & B PHARMACY          THE PRESCRIPTION CENTER
3005 S. LAMAR                      PH. 555-7534
AUSTIN, TX
6330237
                    DR. Hahn
MARIA GARCIA

Take ONE tablet daily.

FERO-FOLIC 500 FILMTABS
ABBOTT / ROSS
STO1554
02/20/93        QTY 100      REFILLS CALL
```

CAUTION: FEDERAL LAW PROHIBITS THE TRANSFER OF THIS DRUG TO ANY PERSON OTHER THAN THE PATIENT FOR WHOM IT WAS PRESCRIBED.

B. Read the questions and write the answers.

1. How many of these tablets should Maria take daily?

   _____

2. What should Maria do to get more of these tablets?

   _____

   _____

3. How many tablets are in the bottle? How do you know that?

   _____

   _____

4. The doctor gave Maria these tablets because she was feeling tired. Maria's father has been feeling tired, too. Should he take some of Maria's tablets? Why or why not?

   _____

   _____

Instructor's Notes: Read the new words and each set of directions with students. Read and discuss the label with students. Help students answer the questions. Use the Unit 4 Review on page 107 to conclude the unit. Then assign *Reading for Today Workbook Four*, Unit 4.

DISCUSSION

Remember

Look at the picture. Who did you grow up with in your community? Was everyone alike?

Predict

Look at the picture and the story title. What do you think this story is about?

Instructor's Notes: Read the discussion questions with students. Discuss the story title and the situation in the picture.

Who Are They?

The people of our land are all different, and that is one of the best things about a big country. We could learn a lot from being together. Then why do we always want to be with people who are like we are? We see someone with different skin and we may not want to be friends. Disabled people may feel that they are not treated the same in a group. People from the country may think they don't like people from the city. It might not be right, but sometimes we don't feel at home with people who are different from us.

Should things be this way? Our country has room for many different groups. We may think they are different, but our daily lives are alike in many ways.

The men and women in the Baker family are from a small city. The families there all do things together, and they are not used to seeing new people. Maybe that is why things got out of hand that hot day in June. Two families were having an outing by the lake. By sundown, there was a big problem.

Instructor's Notes: Have students read silently. Have them underline words they don't recognize. Review the underlined words.

63

Review Words

A. Check the words you know.

☐ 1. bag ☐ 2. took ☐ 3. player

☐ 4. were ☐ 5. hip ☐ 6. camera

☐ 7. truck ☐ 8. day ☐ 9. sundown

☐ 10. tapes ☐ 11. June ☐ 12. different

B. Read and write the sentences. Circle the review words.

1. In June, my wife and I took the family on an outing.

_____

_____

2. We took two big bags of food, a tape player with tapes, and our camera.

_____

_____

3. When my wife got out of the truck, she slipped and landed on her hip.

_____

_____

C. Match the word and its opposite.

_____ 1. day   a. sunup

_____ 2. sundown   b. alike

_____ 3. different c. gave

_____ 4. took   d. night

Instructor's Notes: Read each set of directions with students. For A, have students read the words aloud and then check known words. Have students practice any unknown words in a notebook or journal.

Sight Words

summer
saw
foreign
around

A. Read the words in color. Then read the sentence.

This summer we saw many foreign cars around the city.

B. Underline the sight words in sentences I–3.

1. Some friends of mine went to a foreign country this summer.

2. They did not know how to get around and had trouble talking to the people there.

3. As soon as they could get around without much help, my friends saw a lot of the city.

C. Write the word that completes each sentence.

saw   Summer   foreign   around

1. _____ is a good time to take a trip.

2. Have you been to a _____ country?

3. On our trip we _____ a lot of new sights.

4. Some people like to take trips where they can go

   _____ together in a small group.

D. Read the sentences. Underline the sight words.

When my family came to this country, it was a foreign land to them. They did not know how to get around in a big city. They were not used to the hot summers. Things were different for them, but they saw this foreign land as a chance for a new life.

Instructor's Notes: Read each set of directions with students. For A, read each sight word aloud. Have students repeat. Point out that the g in foreign is silent, and ei is pronounced like the short i in win.

Sight Words

thank
cook
snack
picnic

A. Read the words in color. Then read the sentence.

We must <u>thank</u> the <u>cook</u> who made the <u>snacks</u> for our <u>picnic</u>.

B. Underline the sight words in sentences 1–4.

1. We found a good cook for the picnic.

2. After we meet the cook, we should thank him for the snacks.

3. When I go to a picnic, I don't mind the bugs.

4. After all, what is a picnic without a big bug or two?

C. Write the word that completes each sentence.

snacks   cook   thank   picnic

1. This summer we have a big family _____ .

2. It's a lot of work to _____ the food for a family group.

3. I should _____ my brothers and sisters for helping me.

4. When can we eat the _____ ?

D. Read the sentences. Underline the sight words.

This summer we all met for a family picnic. The sun was out all day, and the food looked good. We snacked, played baseball, and talked. My brother was the cook for all the food for the picnic. We thanked him for doing a good job.

Instructor's Notes: Read each set of directions with students. For A, read each sight word aloud. Have students repeat.

Sight Words

newcomers
park
grass
jump

A. Read the words in color. Then read the sentences.

We met some <u>newcomers</u> at our picnic in the <u>park</u>. We can't sit on the <u>grass</u>, but the children can run to the lake and <u>jump</u> in the water.

B. Underline the sight words in sentences 1–4.

1. Many people go to the park in the summer.

2. Park rules state people can't walk on the grass.

3. The children can jump in the lake and swim.

4. The newcomers sat at a table by us.

C. Write the word that completes each sentence.

jump   park   grass   newcomers

1. We may see the same families at the _____ .

2. We didn't know the family of _____ .

3. The Baker children wanted to _____ right into the lake for a swim.

4. The park rules say not to sit on the _____ .

D. Read the sentences. Underline the sight words.

People use the park in different ways. Sometimes they have picnics or swim in the lake. Children like to run around on the dock and jump in the cold water. The park is owned by the city, and the rules the city set up help newcomers to the park know what they should do.

Instructor's Notes: Read each set of directions with students. Continue journal writing.

67

Phonics: Consonant Digraphs

A. Listen to the beginning sound in each word below.
Underline the letters that stand for the beginning sound.

ch	**sh**	**shr**
chance	shy	shrug
child	shake	shrink

th	**th**	**wh**
then	thank	when
that	thing	why

B. Make other words with ch, sh, shr, th, and wh. Read and write the words.

–in   **–ine**

ch + in = _____   sh + ine = _____

sh + in = _____   shr + ine = _____

th + in = _____   wh + ine = _____

C. Choose the right word for each sentence below.

1. (shine, shrine) I hoped for the sun to _____ the day we went to the park.

2. (hat, that) We were lucky _____ the sun came out, and we had a good day.

3. (sin, shin) We saw a small child fall down and hit her _____ on the rocks.

4. (thin, think) I don't _____ she was hurt.

Instructor's Notes: Read each set of directions with students. For A, have students read the words aloud and listen for the beginning sounds. Explain that certain consonant letters together (*ch, sh, wh, th,* and *shr*) make new sounds. Explain that the *th* digraph stands for two different sounds as in *then* and *thank*.

Phonics: –ack and –ank

–ack
snack
back
pack
sack

A. Read the words in color. Write other –ack words.

bl + ack = _____

sh + ack = _____

st + ack = _____

tr + ack = _____

B. Write an –ack word to finish each sentence.

1. The Baker family will _____ a picnic bag.

2. They carry the food to the park in a big _____ .

3. They like to go _____ to the old tables by the lake.

–ank
thank
bank
sank

C. Read the words in color. Write other –ank words.

bl + ank = _____

dr + ank = _____

fr + ank = _____

D. Write an –ank word to finish each sentence.

1. Mrs. Baker likes to sit by the _____ of the lake.

2. The children _____ cold water when they got hot.

3. Reed dropped his radio in the water and it

_____ .

Instructor's Notes: Show students the *–ack* word pattern in the known sight word *snack* and the *–ank* word pattern in the known sight word *thank*. Explain that both patterns have the short *a* sound. Read each set of directions with students.

Language: Suffixes –ful and –ness

help + ful = helpful   good + ness = goodness

A suffix is a word part added to the end of a word that changes the meaning of the word. The suffix –ful usually means "filled with." Adding –ness to a word changes the word from a describing word to a naming word.

A. Add the suffix and write each new word.

Add –ness	Add –ful
1. still _____	1. thank _____
2. neat _____	2. play _____
3. sad _____	3. use _____
4. sick _____	4. hand _____
5. shy _____	5. hope _____

B. Read the paragraph. Underline the words with –ful and –ness.

I'm hopeful that we'll have a good day for our picnic. The children will be playful in the park. I've told them to be helpful when we get there. I'm glad that sickness didn't keep the family at home.

C. Write the word that completes each sentence.

shyness   thankful   handful   stillness

1. Reed put a _____ of chips on his plate.

2. He has no problem with _____ when meeting new people.

3. We were all _____ for a fun day.

Instructor's Notes: Discuss the examples with students. Read each set of directions with students. For A, have students read the new words. Explain that suffixes add another syllable to each word.

BACK TO THE STORY

■■■■■■■■ **Remember**
What has happened in the story so far?
■■■■■■■■ **Predict**
What can happen when people meet newcomers?

Who Are They?

It was a good day to have a picnic in the park. Because it was hot in June, the Bakers were glad to be by the lake. Before a big family outing like this, Kate Baker always did a lot of shopping. She bought bags and bags of food, with lots of snacks for the children. Because they all liked music, she had someone in the family take a tape player. As she always did, she reminded Jack to get the camera.

When they got to the park, Kate reminded Reed and Nell about the park rules. Jack Baker told his children to come right back to the picnic tables after swimming. Then Kate and Jack let the children run down to the dock and jump in the water. They didn't want the children to get out of sight.

The Bakers were always lucky about getting the picnic tables by the lake. They liked these tables because no one was around. But this summer there were three new tables by the lake. When the Bakers got to the park, a new family was sitting at the tables. From the way they talked, the Bakers could tell they were newcomers.

"I don't like it," Jack said. "Look at them. Look at the way that woman holds her baby on her hip. They are not from this country. I can always tell when someone isn't from around here. I like to know the people who come to this park."

Instructor's Notes: Read the questions with students. Help students review and predict. Then have students read the story silently.

71

Jack was mad about the new family, but he didn't know why. They had three playful children who were running around and yelling. The food they were cooking smelled different, and they had a small foreign car.

The trouble came at sundown when Jack called the children back from the lake. Jack saw that his son Reed was running and yelling. One newcomer, a man, had run after Reed and was holding him down on the grass.

"What are you doing to my son?" Jack yelled. Was the newcomer trying to hurt his son? Then Reed sat up on the grass and Jack saw tape on his hand.

"I fell and cut my hand. This man helped me," Reed said.

"This child cut his hand on the top of an old can," said the newcomer. "It will mend soon. I'm a doctor at the clinic in the city, and I treat many children. He will be OK."

"We can help our own children," Jack said. "What gives you the right to treat my child?"

The helpful newcomer looked at Jack without talking. Then he said, "Maybe I don't have the right to treat this child as mine but, as a doctor, I'm responsible for doing something to help. You have been looking at us all day," he went on. "I know we look different from you, but we like the park, as you do. We like picnics, as you do. And we love children and want to help when they are in trouble. I can see you feel the same way.

Jack looked down. "You're right. I should thank you for helping Reed. Thank goodness you are a doctor! Will you shake my hand?"

"Yes," the man said, and they both laughed. After that, Mrs. Baker took some food to the new family. The children skipped around the tables. The parents could see that the children got used to playing together in no time at all.

Comprehension

Think About It

1. How does Jack feel about people who are newcomers to this country?
2. Why does Jack get mad at the man who ran after his son?
3. Does Jack change his mind about newcomers? What makes you think so?
4. Sum up what happened in the story.

Write About It

Write about a newcomer's feelings. The newcomer can be you or someone else.

Instructor's Notes: Help students read and answer the questions. **Write About It** can be used as a writing or discussion assignment.

73

Comprehension: Sequence

Tips on Sequence

Sequence is about time. It means the 1-2-3 order in which things happen.

Use these tips to find the sequence of events in a story.

1. Look for time words like *before, when, after, then, always, soon.*
2. Look for words that end in –ed. They tell what happened before (in the past).

   Example: The children jumped in the water.

A. Write I, 2, and 3 to show the order in which things happened in the story.

_____ Reed fell and cut his hand.

_____ The Bakers saw a new family sitting at the picnic tables.

_____ Kate Baker bought lots of snacks.

B. Underline the words that complete each sentence.

1. The Baker children learned the park rules
   a. after Reed fell down.
   b. before Kate and Jack let them run to the dock.
   c. when they went shopping with Mrs. Baker.

2. Mrs. Baker took some food to the new family
   a. before sundown.
   b. when she saw the new family at the tables.
   c. after the doctor helped Reed.

Instructor's Notes: Discuss the tips with students. Explain that *sequence* is the same as arranging things in order or listing the steps in how to do something. Then read the directions together.

Life Skill: Reading Park Rules

first

most

other

lifeguard

A. Read the words in color. Then read the rules below.

PARK RULES

1. No picnics on the grass. Use the tables by the lake. Clean up picnic tables after you eat.
2. No running on the dock. Children must mind the lifeguard at all times.
3. No eating or drinking by the water.
4. No yelling or fighting.
5. Don't walk, sit, or smoke on the grass.
6. No cars in the park after 10:00 P.M.

B. Read the questions and write the answers.

1. Do you think most parks have rules like these? Why?

_____

_____

2. What is the first thing parents should do when they take the family to the park?

_____

_____

3. What rules have to do with eating or drinking?

_____

_____

4. What other rules might you see in a park?

_____

Instructor's Notes: Read the new words and each set of directions with students. For B, read and discuss the park rules. Use the Unit 5 Review on page 108 to conclude the unit. Then assign *Reading for Today Workbook Four*, Unit 5.

75

DISCUSSION

Remember

Look at the picture. Do you usually enjoy yourself at parties?

Predict

Look at the picture and the story title. What do you think this story is about?

Instructor's Notes: Read the discussion questions with students. Discuss the story title and the situation in the picture.

Lonely in a Group

I walk from room to room. Sometimes I carry a drink to have something to do with my hands. People walk by me and say, "How are you?" I say, "Fine," but I don't mean it. They might think I'm having a good time, but I'm faking it. I feel shy and lonely.

I don't know one person here but my wife. Unlike me, she knows many people, and they all like her. I can see her laughing and chatting with her boss and some of her friends. I think they are talking about things at work.

I have trouble trying to talk with people I don't know. I feel differently when I'm with my own friends. I feel at home with them because I know they like me.

My wife says that learning to be a good talker is a skill. She tells me not to give up on this problem, but does she know what it's like to be shy? It's like walking down a road with no end in sight. But in time, maybe I'll find a way to get over this problem.

Instructor's Notes: Have students read silently. Have them underline words they don't recognize. Review the underlined words. Have students identify the speaker.

Review Words

A. Check the words you know.

- ☐ 1. road
- ☐ 2. sometimes
- ☐ 3. fine
- ☐ 4. give
- ☐ 5. lonely
- ☐ 6. own
- ☐ 7. wife
- ☐ 8. problem
- ☐ 9. carry
- ☐ 10. does
- ☐ 11. talker
- ☐ 12. person

B. Read and write the sentences. Circle the review words.

1. Sometimes I have problems talking to a person I don't know.

   _____

   _____

2. My own wife tells me I can be a fine talker, but it does not help me.

   _____

   _____

3. Being in a big group gives me a lonely feeling.

   _____

   _____

C. Choose review words to complete the puzzle.

Across
1. take from one spot to another
3. one who talks

Down
2. a street

Instructor's Notes: Read each set of directions with students. For A, have students read the words aloud and then check known words. Have students practice any unknown words in a notebook or journal.

Sight Words

ask
over
would
better

A. Read the words in color. Then read the sentences.

I'll <u>ask</u> my friend Fran to help me get <u>over</u> this problem. Then I <u>would</u> feel <u>better</u> about being in big groups.

B. Underline the sight words in sentences 1–4.

1. I would like to be a better talker.

2. Who can I ask to help me get over this problem?

3. I can ask my friend Fran to help me.

4. I could not ask for a better friend than Fran.

C. Write the word that completes each sentence.

ask   would   over   better

1. I _____ like to have a good time in a group of new people.

2. I can _____ Fran to help me learn how to make new friends.

3. I'll get _____ tips from her.

4. Fran can help me get _____ feeling lonely in a big group.

D. Read the sentences. Underline the sight words.

Would you feel lonely in a big group of people? I would. Fran says I'd better learn to talk. Over and over again she tells me this, "Walk around, and soon you'll meet a person who would like to chat."

Instructor's Notes: Read each set of directions with students. For A, read each sight word aloud. Have students repeat.

Sight Words

bring
every
party
never

A. Read the words in color. Then read the sentence.

My wife brings me to every party, but I never feel like part of the group.

B. Underline the sight words in sentences 1-5.

1. My wife likes to go to every party, big or small.

2. I never want to go to a party where there are lots of people.

3. When I meet new people, I never know what to say.

4. I always feel better when I can bring my wife.

5. For a shy person like me, every party is lonely.

C. Write the word that completes each sentence.

party   every   bring   never

1. I _____ like big parties.

2. I feel like _____ other person here is having a good time.

3. There are a lot of good snacks at this _____ .

4. What snacks did my wife _____ ?

D. Read the sentences. Underline the sight words.

When I'm at a big party, I would like to feel better than I do. Every other person is having a good time, but I'm faking it. Being around people I don't know brings out my shyness. I never know the right thing to say. Does a big party make you feel this way?

Instructor's Notes: Read each set of directions with students. For A, read each sight word aloud. Have students repeat.

Sight Words

join
company
belong
club

A. Read the words in color. Then read the sentences.

I don't <u>join</u> the group at my wife's <u>company</u> party because I feel that I don't <u>belong</u>. It's like a <u>club</u>.

B. Underline the sight words in sentences 1–5.

1. My wife's company gives a big party on a holiday.

2. She always asks me to join her friends from work.

3. They talk about people and things from the company.

4. Because I don't know what they are talking about, I feel that I don't belong there.

5. I must learn how to join the club.

C. Write the word that completes each sentence.

belong   company   join   club

1. My wife works for a good _____ .

2. All the workers feel that they _____ .

3. It's much like joining a _____ .

4. But when you don't work there, you can't always _____ the group.

D. Read the sentences. Underline the sight words.

When my wife's company gives a party, I don't have a good time. I feel like I'm on my own—that I don't belong to the group. I don't know how to join in the fun. Why do I feel that they have a club and I don't belong to it?

Instructor's Notes: Read each set of directions with students. Continue journal writing.

81

Phonics: Silent Letters

A. Listen to the sounds in each word. Underline each letter that stands for no sound, or is silent.

wr	**kn**	**gu**	**gh**
write	know	guitar	right
wrap	knit	guide	knight

B. Make other words with kn or wr. Read and write the words.

kn + it   = _____   wr + ote = _____

kn + ock = _____   wr + ing = _____

kn + ot   = _____   wr + y   = _____

kn + ight = _____   wr + ap = _____

kn + ee   = _____   wr + en = _____

C. Choose the right word for each sentence below.

1. (knock, know) I don't _____ what to say to people at a party.

2. (wring, wrap) I stand at the back of the room and _____ my hands.

3. (knit, knee) I don't fit in with this tightly _____ group of people.

4. (wry, wrap) I hope they _____ up this party; I want to go home.

5. (right, write) I feel like I never say the _____ thing.

Instructor's Notes: Read each set of directions with students. For A, have students read the words aloud. Explain that in some words not all the letters stand for a sound. For example, in the *wr* pattern, the *r* is sounded and the *w* is silent. Students will need to learn to recognize silent letters.

Phonics: –ing and –ub

–ing
bring
king
ring
sing
wing

A. Read the words in color. Write other –ing words.

spr + ing = _____

str + ing = _____

sw + ing = _____

wr + ing = _____

B. Write an –ing word to finish each sentence.

1. Fran knows how to get into the _____ of things at a party.

2. She can _____ and play the guitar.

3. Fran likes to _____ friends to the party.

–ub
club
hub
rub
tub

C. Read the words in color. Write other –ub words.

gr + ub = _____

shr + ub = _____

sn + ub = _____

D. Write a –ub word to finish each sentence.

1. How can I join this _____ ?

2. I feel that the people _____ me.

3. Fran is always at the _____ of the action at a party.

Instructor's Notes: Show students the –ing word pattern in the known sight word *bring* and the –ub word pattern in the known sight word *club*. Explain that both patterns have short vowel sounds (*i* and *u*). Read each set of directions with students.

Language: Abbreviations and Titles

Doctor = Dr.   Company = Co.

> An abbreviation is a short form of a word. Most abbreviations end with a period. An abbreviation that is part of the name of a person or place begins with a capital letter.

A. Read each word and its abbreviation. Write each abbreviation.

Street = St. _____   Road = Rd. _____

Doctor = Dr. _____   Avenue = Ave. _____

ounce = oz. _____   pound = lb. _____

B. Read the paragraph. Underline the abbreviations.

My wife works for the B. D. Clay Co. on Shell Ave. The company has a health plan with Dr. Parker. The doctor works at Pope St. and School Rd. I will see Dr. Parker at the company party on Sunday, June 4.

C. Write the abbreviation for each title or word.

1. Doctor Key _____

2. Land Avenue _____

3. 25 pounds _____

4. Dean Company _____

5. Dune Street _____

6. 5 ounces _____

7. Waters Road _____

Instructor's Notes: Discuss the examples with students. Read each set of directions with students. Read the information about abbreviations to students. Explain that the abbreviated form is said the same as the long form. For example, *St.* is read as *street*.

BACK TO THE STORY

▪▪▪▪▪▪▪▪▪ **Remember**

What has happened in the story so far?

▪▪▪▪▪▪▪▪▪ **Predict**

Do you think a person can get over being shy? If so, how?

Lonely in a Group

Every time my wife's boss gives a company picnic or a party, I have a problem joining the group. Sometimes I feel that I don't belong with people I don't know. My wife knows that I hate going to these parties, but she always wants me to go with her. She is an out-going person, and she can't see why I have trouble talking to people.

I must get over this problem. Then I would not be lonely in a group of new people. I would have a good time and feel that I belong in the company club.

I'll talk with my friend Fran about my shyness. Fran sells homes to people in our city, and she is used to talking to people she does not know. Fran can make friends right away with no trouble. You might say that it's one of her jobs to be a good talker.

• • •

"To make friends, Rick, you have to be a friend. You don't have problems when you are around people you know, do you?" Fran asked.

"No, but then I know they like me," I said. "I keep thinking about that company party. Over and over I couldn't think of the right thing to say. I never want to go back to one again."

"Tell me about it," said Fran. "Maybe I can give you some good tips that work for me."

Instructor's Notes: Read the questions with students. Help students review and predict. Then have students read the story silently.

85

"Sometimes I feel better when I have something to do with my hands. I carry a drink around with me, but at the other party, I spilled it all over the rug. When I try to think of the right thing to say, my mind is blank and the words don't come out right. See what I mean?" I asked.

"OK. Why don't we talk about some better ways to meet people at a party? When a person you don't know sits down by you, what do you say?" Fran asked.

"I try to give them a friendly greeting and tell them my name," I said.

"Is that all?"

"What do you want me to say?" I asked.

"Well, there are some things everyone wants to talk about. Ask about family, work, or school. Or a person may know a lot about something, like baseball or fine music. Another tip is to think about what you can give to a party. I know you can play the guitar well. Why not bring the guitar to the party and ask others to join in the singing? Or bring some games—people of all ages like games. When you are playing a game, you don't have time to think about what to say."

I need to think about Fran's tips. When I go to a party, it does not help to think about how shy I feel. I need to join in the fun, and then think less about my own problems. Every party would be a chance to meet new people. After all, there might be other people in the group who feel shy, too. Maybe we could make our own club!

After talking with Fran, I think I'm on the right road to overcoming my shyness. I'll never need to feel lonely in a group again.

Comprehension

Think About It

1. How does Rick feel when he goes to parties?
2. How is Rick's wife different from him?
3. What advice does Fran give Rick?
4. Sum up what happened in the story.

Write About It

When do you feel shy or lonely? What do you do to feel less shy or lonely?

Instructor's Notes: Help students read and answer the questions. **Write About It** can be used as a writing or discussion assignment.

Comprehension: Context

A. Read the sentence. Answer the questions about the new word.

Fran will <u>invite</u> all her friends to her party.

1. Could it mean <u>remember</u>? _____ (Clue: That word would not make sense in the sentence.)

2. Could it mean <u>ask</u>? _____ (That makes sense.)

B. The paragraph below has two words that you may not know. Use context to decide what the words mean.

Rick has trouble talking to people he does not know. You could say he is a <u>bashful</u> person. He can't think of the right things to say. Maybe these people won't like him. Maybe they would like to spend time with other friends. The more Rick thinks about these things, the more shy he becomes. He doesn't <u>enjoy</u> being shy.

1. A bashful person is _____ .
   bossy   shy   tired

2. Enjoy means to _____ .
   like   need   want

Life Skill: Coping with Shyness

list
attention
relax
wrong

A. Read the words in color. Then read the tips below.

How to Cope with Shyness

1. Look right at a friendly face when you are talking before a group. Think about the worst mistake you could make and laugh about it. Ask "If I flub a line in my talk, will everyone get up and walk out? No!"

2. Don't make up for shyness by being bossy. You may not want others to know how you feel, but being bossy isn't good.

3. Get other people to talk. Then stop thinking about you and pay attention to what they are saying.

4. Don't make up for shyness by drinking too much. You may think it will help you talk, but you'll say the wrong thing.

5. Relax! There will be other shy people around. You are more like other people than you are different.

B. Read the questions and write the answers.

1. Most of the list tells you what to do about shyness. Which sentences tell you what not to do?

_____

2. Which three things in the list might be the most helpful to you? Why?

_____

_____

3. Tip #5 says, "You are more like other people than you are different." What does this sentence mean?

_____

_____

Instructor's Notes: Read the new words and each set of directions with students. Read and discuss the tips with students. Help students answer the questions. Use the Unit 6 Review on page 109 to conclude the unit. Then assign *Reading for Today Workbook Four*, Unit 6.

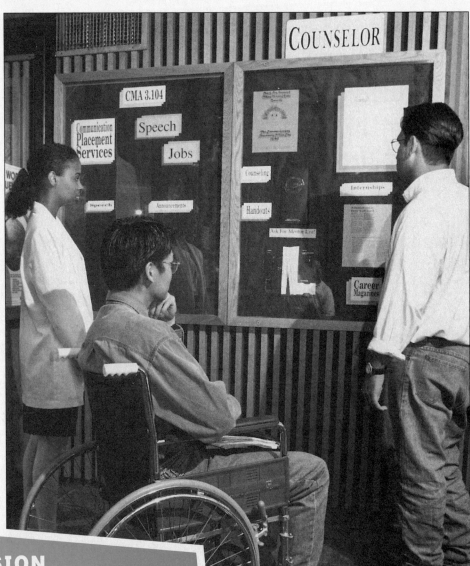

DISCUSSION

Remember

Look at the picture. How have you or someone you know looked for a job?

Predict

Look at the picture and the story title. What do you think this story is about?

Instructor's Notes: Read the discussion questions with students. Discuss the story title and the situation in the picture.

Can I Begin Again?

I won't forget that cold day for a long time. I got to work, and there were the words "For Rent" on Jill's store.

"What's this about?" I asked Jill.

"I'm getting out before I lose money," said Jill. "The rent is too much. I'll look for a different store that's not in this city."

"Well, what do I do for a job?" I asked.

"I can't help you there, Jim," said Jill. "Ask around. Look at the want ads or talk to some friends. Maybe you can find some work at another store."

"No, never again," I said. "I'm tired of going from one job to another. I want a job I can stay with for a long time, maybe with a big company."

"Well, good luck, Jim," said Jill. "I'll send you back pay when I get around to it."

The day had gotten much colder!

Instructor's Notes: Have students read silently. Have them underline words they don't recognize. Review the underlined words. Have students identify the character Jim.

Review Words

A. Check the words you know.

☐ 1. join ☐ 2. responsible ☐ 3. school

☐ 4. company ☐ 5. back ☐ 6. list

☐ 7. learn ☐ 8. new ☐ 9. plan

☐ 10. around ☐ 11. want ☐ 12. over

B. Read and write the sentences. Circle the review words.

1. I would like to learn a responsible job and join a big company.

_____

2. I know I need to learn more about how to look for a good job.

_____

3. I'll look over the want ads, ask around, and make a list of where to look.

_____

4. I might need to think about going back to school.

_____

C. Read the clues. Choose a review word for the answer.

1. belong to _____

2. find out _____

3. not old _____

4. outline _____

 Instructor's Notes: Read each set of directions with students. For A, have students read the words aloud and then check known words. Have students practice any unknown words in a notebook or journal.

Sight Words

now
center
keep
year

A. Read the words in color. Then read the sentences.

Maybe <u>now</u> I should talk to someone at the learning <u>center</u>. They <u>keep</u> job listings up <u>year</u> round.

B. Underline the sight words in sentences 1–4.

1. The city runs the learning center.

2. Bill has worked at the center for a year.

3. He keeps telling me I need a year of school.

4. I should try going back to school now.

C. Write the word that completes each sentence.

now   center   keep   year

1. I can't _____ going from job to job.

2. I need to find a better job _____ .

3. The people at the learning _____ can help me.

4. They tell me I can learn new skills in a _____ or less.

D. Read the sentences. Underline the sight words.

Bill has been at the center for a year now. He can go to school and work at the same time. He keeps trying to get me to come in and talk to someone at the center. Maybe now that my job with Jill is over I will. Now is a good time of year to begin over.

Instructor's Notes: Read each set of directions with students. For A, read each sight word aloud. Have students repeat.

93

Sight Words

once
listen
train
your

A. Read the words in color. Then read the sentence.

Once I sat down to listen to Bill, he told me how the city can train you to update your job skills.

B. Underline the sight words in sentences 1–4.

1. Once you get into the center, you make money as you train.

2. This school is different from the ones I once went to.

3. The people at the center ask about your skills and what you like to do.

4. I'm glad Bill made me listen to him.

C. Write the word that completes each sentence.

train   listen   Your   Once

1. I can still make money as I _____ for a job.

2. _____ friends can be helpful in finding a job.

3. It pays to _____ to the right people.

4. _____ I get into the center, I should like it.

D. Read the sentences. Underline the sight words.

Bill said, "Listen, the center can help you. You can train for a job and go to school at the same time. The city has joined together with companies that train people. Once you get into the center, they listen to your job needs, and then get you a job. You make money as you learn and train."

 Instructor's Notes: Read each set of directions with students. For A, read each sight word aloud. Have students repeat.

Sight Words

straight
career
careful
customers

A. Read the words in color. Then read the sentences.

Can I go straight from this school into a career? I'll have to do a careful job and work well with customers.

B. Underline the sight words in sentences 1–4.

1. I wanted to begin a career at Jill's shop.

2. She saw that I was careful with the TV sets and radios.

3. Some days I worked straight from 8 A.M. to 6 P.M.

4. I didn't get to meet many of Jill's customers.

C. Write the word that completes each sentence.

customers   career   straight   careful

1. I went _____ to the center.

2. They looked at my work record and asked how

   I would talk to _____ .

3. I was _____ in filling out the list of things they asked me.

4. This is my chance to plan for a good _____ .

D. Read the sentences. Underline the sight words.

On my first day at the center, I was sent straight to Mr. Teller at his shop. His customers have car radios, TVs, and CD players they bring in. Mr. Teller looked straight at me. He told me if I'm as careful as he thinks I am, I can do well in this career.

Instructor's Notes: Read each set of directions with students. Continue journal writing.

95

Phonics: y as a Vowel

why   baby

y = long i   y = long e

A. Read the words and listen for the last vowel sound. Write the word and circle the letter that stands for the last sound.

1. why _____   1. lucky _____

2. my _____   2. carry _____

3. by _____   3. party _____

4. dry _____   4. lonely _____

B. Read the words. Then write each word under the right heading.

sly   y = long i   y = long e

try

baby   1. _____   1. _____

healthy

cry   2. _____   2. _____

many

heavy   3. _____   3. _____

fly   4. _____   4. _____

C. Read the sentences. Circle the y words with the long i sound. Underline the y words with the long e sound.

I've had many jobs over the years. I'm lucky to have a chance to try a new school. I don't know why my old school didn't work for me. Now I can train for a good career and make money at the same time.

Instructor's Notes: Read each set of directions with students. Explain that the *y* can stand for the long *i* sound at the end of one-syllable words or the long *e* sound at the end of words with more than one syllable.

Phonics: –eep and –ear

–eep
deep
jeep
keep
weep

A. Read the words in color. Write other –eep words.

sh + eep = _____

sl + eep = _____

st + eep = _____

sw + eep = _____

B. Write an –eep word to finish each sentence.

1. I will work to _____ this job with Mr. Teller.

2. The costs of other training schools are _____ .

3. I know, down _____ , that I can do well at the center.

–ear
year
dear
fear
hear
near

C. Read the words in color. Write other –ear words.

cl + ear = _____

sh + ear = _____

sm + ear = _____

sp + ear = _____

D. Write an –ear word to finish each sentence.

1. Mr. Teller's company is _____ my home.

2. I will listen well and _____ what Mr. Teller tells me to do.

3. What I want to do with my life is much more

_____ than it was a year ago.

Instructor's Notes: Show students the *–eep* word pattern in the known sight word *keep* and the *–ear* word pattern in the known sight word *year*. Explain that both patterns have the long *e* vowel sound. Read each set of directions with students.

Language: Days and Months

January = Jan.   Sunday = Sun.

The name of each day of the week and month of the year begins with a capital letter. You can write the days and most of the months in a short form. These abbreviations begin with a capital letter and end with a period.

A. Read each word and its abbreviation. Write the abbreviations.

Sunday   = Sun. _____   Thursday = Thurs. _____

Monday   = Mon. _____   Friday   = Fri. _____

Tuesday   = Tues. _____   Saturday = Sat. _____

Wednesday = Wed. _____

B. Read each word and its abbreviation. Write the short forms.

January   = Jan. _____   August   = Aug. _____

February   = Feb. _____   September = Sept. _____

March   = Mar. _____   October   = Oct. _____

April   = Apr. _____   November = Nov. _____

May, June, July   December = Dec. _____

C. Read the paragraph. Underline the names of months and days.

It was a cold Monday in December when I saw "For Rent" on Jill's store. I went to look for a job on Wednesday, Thursday, and Friday. All the people said, "We have no work for you. Try again in January, February, or March." On Saturday and Sunday I sat home and moped, but I'll try again on Monday.

Instructor's Notes: Discuss the examples with students. Explain that the abbreviation is said the same as the complete word. For example, *Sun.* is read as *Sunday*. Read each set of directions with students. Note that *May*, *June*, and *July* have no short forms.

BACK TO THE STORY

Remember
What has happened in the story so far?

Predict
Look at the picture. What do you think will happen in the rest of the story?

Can I Begin Again?

Once I got used to going to school again, it was OK. I spend three days a week working at Mr. Teller's shop. The boss put me to work first on TV sets. That's the work I know best. I think he wanted to see what I could do.

Instructor's Notes: Read the questions with students. Help students review and predict. Then have students read the story silently.

99

Mr. Teller would walk by from time to time and look over my work. I saw he was making notes about it, and that got me upset.

"Listen," said the boss, "keep in mind that job training here is like going to school. In a way, I'm like your teacher. I have to keep a careful record of your work this year. I'll grade you on your work and how you're getting along on the job."

I work at Mr. Teller's shop on Monday, Wednesday, and Friday. I go to school at the learning center on Tuesday and Thursday. I thought I had learned a lot working for Jill, but I'm still learning something new all the time. My math and reading skills have gotten better along with my skills on the job. I know now that training on the job will help me in getting the career I want. I make money as I work. I get grades for all the work I do at Mr. Teller's and at the learning center.

I see Bill on the days I go to the learning center. I'm glad I listened to him about looking into the center when I was out of work. He told me the center would help me look at school differently and he was right. Sometimes you have to give some things another chance. They can work out better than you thought.

● ● ●

As time went by, things began to work out for me in a big way. Mr. Teller began to train me to work on other jobs that needed attention, not just TVs. I was glad that I was moving on to new skills.

One Tuesday I saw Mr. Teller heading straight for me. My first thought was, "I hope I didn't do something wrong!" I quickly thought about all the jobs I had worked on that day. Had I remembered to be as careful as I should have been?

The boss said, "Jim, today I'm putting you at the Customer Desk. I have a feeling you'll do a careful job there."

Well, now I had the chance to talk to customers about different problems they had. As I talked to customers one by one, I felt better about my skills in working with people and helping them with their problems.

At the end of the day, Mr. Teller said, "Listen, Jim, I like the way you work. You've learned to do many different things this company wants and needs. I hope you'll think about a career here when you get out of school at the end of the year."

"Does that mean you're giving me an *A*, Mr. Teller?" I asked.

"You bet!" he said.

I don't know whose grin was bigger, his or mine!

Comprehension

Think About It

1. What surprised Jim about going back to school?
2. Why did Jim want to work for Mr. Teller?
3. Why did Jim's skills get better as he worked?
4. Sum up what happened in the story.

Write About It

How would you feel if you had to begin again and train for a new job?

Instructor's Notes: Help students read and answer the questions. **Write About It** can be used as a writing or discussion assignment.

101

Comprehension: Drawing Conclusions

> **Tips for Drawing Conclusions**
>
> A **conclusion** is an opinion you form after putting facts together. A conclusion is usually not stated in a story. You have to come up with it yourself by *reading between the lines.*
>
> **Use these tips to draw a conclusion.**
> 1. Read the story or paragraph.
> 2. Keep the facts in mind. List them.
> 3. Think about what the facts say to you.
> 4. Draw a conclusion based on the facts and their meaning for you.

A. Read this paragraph.

Fay trained for a new job and went to school at the same time. She got her pay at the end of the week if she did good work or not. Why should she do her best? Sometimes she was late for work. Her boss didn't ask her to stay with the company when the training ended.

B. Find four facts and list them.

Fact 1 _____

Fact 2 _____

Fact 3 _____

Fact 4 _____

C. Which is the best conclusion to draw? Circle it.

1. Fay is not in the right job.

2. Fay has a bad life at home.

3. The boss didn't like Fay's looks.

Instructor's Notes: Discuss the tips with students. Discuss what *reading between the lines* means. Then read the directions together.

Life Skill: Reading a Schedule

schedule
assignment
lunch
complaint

A. Read the words in color. Then read the work schedule and assignments.

❖ TELLER'S TV SHOP ❖						
WORK SCHEDULE AND ASSIGNMENTS						
	8:00–10:00 AM	10:00–NOON	12:00–1:00 PM	1:00–2:00 PM	2:00–3:00 PM	3:00–4:00 PM
Jim	TVs	Car Radios	LUNCH	Customer Desk	Customer Desk	CDs
Belle	Car Radios	CDs	Customer Desk	LUNCH	TVs	Help with records
Matt	CDs	Customer Desk	LUNCH	TVs	Car Radios	Car Radios
April	Customer Desk	TVs	VCRs	LUNCH	CDs	Customer Desk
NOTE: See Mr. Teller if you have customer complaints.						

B. Read the questions and write the answers.

1. a. When do workers begin their work day? _____

   b. When do they end their day? _____

2. a. When does Jim start work at the Customer Desk?

   _____

   b. When does he stop work at the Customer Desk?

   _____

3. What work does April do first every day?

   _____

4. Why do you think workers are scheduled for

   different lunch times? _____

   _____

   _____

Instructor's Notes: Read the new words and each set of directions with students. Help them read the work schedule and answer the questions. Use the Unit 7 Review on page 110 to conclude the unit. Then assign *Reading for Today Workbook Four*, Unit 7.

103

Unit 1 Review

A. Write the word that completes each sentence.

law	been	Native American	here
elected	senator	horse	ranch
put	silver	jewelry	again

1. Senator Campbell was _____ by the people.

2. He owns a _____ and makes _____ .

3. Ben Nighthorse is his _____ name.

4. Campbell may be elected _____ in 1996.

B. Write the word under the correct heading.

lovely   letter   make   silver
congress   luck   worked   puts

One-Syllable Words   **Two-Syllable Words**

1. _____   1. _____

2. _____   2. _____

3. _____   3. _____

4. _____   4. _____

C. Write the word that fits best in each sentence.

1. The silver jewelry that Campbell makes is _____ .
                                          handy   lovely

2. He works on the jewelry _____ .
                          nightly   timely

3. Campbell gives time and money to _____ causes.
                                  mighty   needy

Unit 2 Review

A. Write the word that completes each sentence.

roommate	save	less	spend
coupons	then	why	think
could	cost	too	much

1. Cutting out _____ can take a lot of time.

2. _____ they help us save on something we need?

3. My _____ says that coupons can help us save money.

4. Do you _____ my roommate is right about coupons?

B. Write –ink or –y to make new words. Write the word that fits best in each sentence.

1. wh + _____ = _____   _____ did I buy all this pop?

2. dr + _____ = _____   I can't _____ all of it.

3. tr + _____ = _____   I'll _____ to take some back.

4. th + _____ = _____   Do you _____ the store will take some back?

C. Write the word that fits best in each sentence.

1. Someone at the store _____ my roommate a new radio.
   sell   sold

2. The trouble was that Kay _____ too much for it.
   paid   pay

3. It _____ me mad to find out that my sister _____ a lot of money.
   make   made   spent   spend

A. Write the word that completes each sentence.

always	meet	or	after
school	soon	means	where
report	must	card	grades

1. Mr. Sanders _____ wanted to learn to read well.

2. He wants Jay to get good _____ in reading.

3. That _____ Jay will have to do all his homework.

4. Jay _____ come home right _____ school.

B. Write -eet or -ean to make new words. Write the word that fits best in each sentence.

1. m + _____ = _____ Mr. Sanders will _____ Jay's teacher.

2. gr + _____ = _____ She will _____ him with a handshake.

3. J + _____ = _____ Jay's teacher is Mrs. _____ Keating.

4. m + _____ = _____ She isn't a _____ teacher.

C. Write the word that fits best in each sentence.

1. A person who can't read is _____ about some things.
   unclear   unloved

2. Jay must _____ things many times.
   rerun   reread

3. I'll _____ Jay to do his homework.
   repay   remind

4. Jay thinks he is _____ to have lots of homework.
   unlucky   unsold

Unit 4 Review

A. Write the word that completes each sentence.

know	tired	late	before
rock	small	new	pregnant
wife	baby	as	responsible

1. My _____ and I will soon be parents.

2. We're both _____ for looking after the baby.

3. _____ the baby comes, I'll need to learn many things.

4. Is there a school for _____ parents?

B. Write _–ate_ or _–ock_ to make new words. Write the word that fits best in each sentence.

1. pl + _____ = _____ A new baby can't eat from a _____ .

2. bl + _____ = _____ Babies like to play with this _____ .

3. l + _____ = _____ Will Carlos have to get up _____ at night?

4. r + _____ = _____ He may have to _____ the baby.

C. Add _–ies_ to the words. Write the word that completes each sentence.

baby _____   family _____

cry _____   country _____

1. We know that our _____ will be glad about the baby.

2. We won't mind when the baby's _____ wake us.

3. Someday we want to have more _____ .

4. Many _____ have laws that help children.

A. Write the word that completes each sentence.

around	park	thank	foreign
summer	cook	grass	snacks
picnic	jump	newcomers	saw

1. On a summer day, many people go to the _____ .

2. We see families we know and some _____ .

3. The children can run _____ and play games.

4. When they get hot, they can _____ in the lake and swim.

B. Write _-ack_ or _-ank_ to make new words. Write the word that fits best in each sentence.

1. p + _____ = _____   The Baker family will _____ a big picnic bag.

2. b + _____ = _____   They'll go _____ to the old tables by the lake.

3. th + _____ = _____   Who can we _____ for cooking all the food?

4. b + _____ = _____   We can sit on the _____ of the lake.

C. Write the word that fits best in each sentence.

1. We were _____ the sun was out all day.
   hopeful   thankful

2. Thank _____ Dad has a big van.
   goodness   sickness

3. I'm lucky to have _____ children.
   helpful   playful

Unit 6 Review

A. Write the word that completes each sentence.

club	every	ask	better
join	party	would	belong
over	bring	never	company

1. I _____ can relax at big parties.

2. I _____ like to have a good time in a group of new people.

3. Somehow I feel like I don't _____ .

4. _____ time I try to say something, the words come out wrong.

B. Write –ub or –ing to make new words. Write the word that fits best in each sentence.

1. cl + _____ = _____   Why did I join this _____ ?

2. sn + _____ = _____   Maybe the people here will not

   _____ me.

3. sw + _____ = _____   I need to learn how to get in the

   _____ of things.

4. br + _____ = _____   Maybe it would help to _____
   some of my own friends.

C. Draw lines to match the words and abbreviations.

1. Street   oz.
2. pound   Dr.
3. Avenue   St.
4. ounces   Ave.
5. Doctor   lb.

Unit 7 Review

A. Write the word that completes each sentence.

keep	center	now	year
listen	your	train	once
straight	career	careful	customers

1. Bill told Jim about the learning _____ .

2. Jim found out he can _____ there for a new job.

3. Jim works for Mr. Teller _____ .

4. He works on TVs and radios that _____ bring in.

B. Write –ear or –eep to make new words. Write the word that fits best in each sentence.

1. y + _____ = _____   Bill has been at the center for a

   _____ .

2. d + _____ = _____   The letter began "_____ Jim."

3. n + _____ = _____   The company is _____ Jim's home.

4. k + _____ = _____   Jim needs a job he can _____ .

C. Draw lines to match the words and abbreviations.

1. Wednesday   Dec.
2. February   Apr.
3. Tuesday   Thurs.
4. December   Wed.
5. Thursday   Tues.
6. April   Feb.

Answer Key

● ● ● ● ●

Unit 1

▶ **Page 8**

A. Answers will vary.

B. 1. Ben Nighthorse Campbell takes (action) in (many) (different) ways.
2. Campbell (still) (does) a job he learned as a (child).
3. He is good at (working) (together) with (different) (people).
4. Campbell (holds) down (more) than one job (because) he can do many things well.

C. 1. different
2. many
3. working

▶ **Page 9**

B. 1. Ben Nighthorse Campbell is a <u>Native</u> <u>American</u>.
2. He has <u>been</u> of help to people with problems.
3. Campbell works to make bills into <u>laws</u>.
4. <u>Native</u> <u>Americans</u> want action on these <u>laws</u>.
5. There have <u>been</u> problems about the water rights of different groups of people <u>here</u> in the U.S.

C. 1. here
2. Native Americans
3. been
4. laws

D. The land and water in the U.S. are different from when <u>Native</u> <u>Americans</u> owned the land. People came to the U.S. to make homes in this country and took a lot of the land. They have used up or hurt the water in some way. Campbell feels that people can work to make <u>laws</u> that fix these problems.

▶ **Page 10**

B. 1. People <u>elected</u> Campbell because he is a man of action.
2. A <u>senator</u> is elected to help make laws.
3. <u>Senator</u> Campbell owns and runs a <u>horse</u> <u>ranch</u> as well.

C. 1. elected
2. senator
3. ranch
4. horses

D. At his <u>ranch</u>, <u>Senator</u> Campbell can ride <u>horses</u> and work with his <u>ranch</u> hands. He doesn't have the time for his <u>ranch</u> that he used to, but he gets there when he can. He gives his job as <u>senator</u> his all because he was <u>elected</u> by the people.

▶ **Page 11**

B. 1. Campbell learned how to make <u>jewelry</u> when he was a child.
2. Campbell's teacher in <u>jewelry</u> making was his father.
3. He sometimes <u>puts</u> stones in his <u>silver</u> <u>jewelry</u>.
4. People who like his work come to him for <u>jewelry</u> <u>again</u>.

C. 1. puts
2. silver
3. again
4. jewelry

D. Will Campbell find time to make more <u>silver</u> <u>jewelry</u>? He says he won't give up doing work he likes this well. He works on the <u>silver</u> <u>jewelry</u> at night. That way he can go to his job as senator <u>again</u> in the daytime and still <u>put</u> in time on what he likes, making <u>silver</u> <u>jewelry</u>.

▶ **Page 12**

B. One Syllable   Two Syllables
1. law	1. problem
2. more	2. rancher
3. group	3. safety
4. own	4. father
5. like	5. country

C. 1. Ben Campbell holds down many jobs.

    2. Campbell owns a horse ranch.

    3. Sometimes he works with silver.

    4. He puts in time working for people.

▶ **Page 13**

B. wallet—2   different—3   someone—2

    plan—1   learned—1   uniform—3

    value—2   street—1   video—3

D. again—a   doctor—o   parent—e

    holiday—i   problem—e   person—e

▶ **Page 14**

A.
1. differently	1. needy
2. lovely	2. handy
3. safely	3. hilly
4. likely	4. lucky
5. nightly	5. mighty

B.   Campbell does things differently. He holds down more than one job, and he works for needy causes. The people are lucky that they elected him senator. His friendly ways are likely to get him elected again.

C. 1. nightly

    2. lovely

    3. handy

▶ **Page 17**

Think About It

Discuss your answers with your instructor.

    1. He works to get action taken on problems. He knows how to do many things well and knows how to talk to people.

    2. Answers will vary. Possible answers include helping make laws, talking to people about problems, serving on groups or committees in the Senate.

    3. He makes silver jewelry and raises horses.

    4. Summaries should include his many activities as senator, craftsman, and rancher, as well as his interest in the world at large and people in general.

Write About It

Discuss your writing with your instructor.

▶ **Page 18**

A. 3

B. 1

C. Since Campbell is a Native American, he took the name Ben Nighthorse.

▶ **Page 19**

B. 1. b

    2. c

    3. a

C. Discuss your letter with your instructor.

Unit 2

▶ **Page 22**

A. Answers will vary.

B. 1. Buyers like Kay want all the things they see.

    2. Do they buy because they need all these things?

    3. Kay doesn't need many of the things she buys.

4. Store owners can make money when they (sell) to (buyers) like Kay.

C. 1. baseball
2. seven
3. game

▶ **Page 23**

B. 1. I read the ads and then clip out the coupons.
2. Do I need to save all the coupons I see?
3. Could they help me save on something I need?
4. I could clip out the coupons I want to use.
5. Then I could use the coupons to get the things I need.

C. 1. could   2. coupons
3. then   4. save

D.   Nan and Kay want to save money when they shop. One way they could save money is to use coupons. Nan finds coupons in the store ads, and then Kay clips out the ones that could help them save. They save a lot of coupons and then buy the things they need.

▶ **Page 24**

B. 1. Many people could pay less using coupons, but they don't think about it.
2. The right way to use coupons is to think about what you are buying.
3. How much money does meat cost without the coupon?
4. Will meat cost more or less at a different store?

C. 1. less   2. think
3. much   4. cost

D.   Food costs more and more these days. I think we could save money by using coupons. But we have to think about some things

when we shop. How much does food cost when we use coupons? Will the cost be less at a big store that has a lot of goods? How much trouble is it to get to that store?

▶ **Page 25**

B. 1. My roommate saves all the coupons she sees.
2. Then she spends money for things we don't need.
3. When we shop together, she doesn't buy too much.
4. Why can't she do that when I'm not with her?
5. I think my roommate could learn to stop buying things we don't need.

C. 1. Why   2. too
3. roommate   4. spend

D.   My roommate has a problem when she goes shopping without me. She spends money on things we don't need because she thinks she saves money. Then we have too many things, but not what we need. Why do store ads and coupons make people want things they can't use? I'm going to help my roommate quit buying things we don't need.

▶ **Page 26**

A. brand   cream   drive   friend
brag   crop   drop   from
gray   prison   truck   strap
group   problem trouble street

B. gray   drip
fray   grip
tray   strip
stray   trip

C. 1. brag   2. trip
3. brand   4. tray

▶ **Page 27**

A. cry, dry, fry, try

B. I. my

2. try

3. why

C. wink, brink, drink

D. I. drink

2. drink

3. think

▶ **Page 28**

B. I gave some coupons to my roommate, and she took them to the store. Kay thought all the coupons were good, and she bought a lot of things. Then she found out the coupons were good in May, but not in June. I hope this taught Kay to read coupons well.

C. I. sold

2. paid

▶ **Page 31**

Think About It

Discuss your answers with your instructor.

I. They wanted to get enough coupons from the packages to send them in and win tickets to a baseball game.

2. They won more hot dogs.

3. She found out that using coupons doesn't always save money. She learned that she sometimes bought something she didn't really need just because she had a coupon.

4. Summaries should include the fact that the roommates have different ideas about using coupons. Kay buys whatever she has coupons for and Nan thinks she shouldn't do that. Nan tries her own way of using coupons, but her plan doesn't work either. The roommates learn they need to think about which coupons they use.

Write About It

Discuss your writing with your instructor.

▶ **Page 32**

B. Fact 1: Matt looked at the coupons.

Fact 2: They were for tea bags.

Fact 3: Matt gave the coupons to Kay.

Fact 4: She used them when she went to the store.

C. 3. Kay likes tea.

▶ **Page 33**

B. I. coupon 1

2. Oz. stands for the word ounce.

3. coupon 1, 50¢; coupon 2, 15¢

Unit 3

▶ **Page 36**

A. Answers will vary.

B. I. Will Jay be (upset) because I can't (teach) him to read?

2. I (gave) him help with baseball, but (who) will be his reading (teacher)?

3. When Jay (takes) time with his work, he does not get (into) trouble.

4. We'll all work (together) to help Jay (learn) to read.

C. I. b

2. c

3. a

▶ **Page 37**

B. I. Mr. Sanders always wanted to go to school.

2. Going to school means you have a chance to learn.

3. Schools are not always for children.

4. A teacher must spend a lot of time helping people learn.

5. Does our teacher <u>mean</u> that we <u>must</u> <u>always</u> do well?

C. 1. school   2. always
    3. must   4. mean

D.   Some parents think <u>schools</u> <u>must</u> <u>always</u> teach children to read. But children <u>must</u> get help at home with the things they learn at <u>school</u>. What does this <u>mean</u> for parents who can't read well? Sometimes these parents <u>must</u> get help, too.

▶ **Page 38**

B. 1. Mr. Sanders must <u>meet</u> his son's teacher <u>soon</u>.
    2. Jay told his father <u>where</u> to find the teacher.
    3. Mrs. Keating said she will <u>meet</u> Mr. Sanders.
    4. <u>Soon</u> he will talk to her about Jay's problem.
    5. <u>After</u> this talk, Mr. Sanders will help Jay.

C. 1. after   2. meet
    3. soon   4. Where

D.   Parents may have problems to work out when they <u>meet</u> with a teacher. They must find out <u>where</u> the school is. Sometimes both the child and parents must find a time to <u>meet</u> together with the teacher. Parents might need to be at home <u>soon</u> <u>after</u> work. But, when parents and teachers find time for these <u>meetings</u>, they can work out ways to help a child.

▶ **Page 39**

B. 1. In school you may have to give a <u>report</u>.
    2. Will you get a good <u>or</u> bad <u>grade</u>?
    3. A <u>report</u> that makes the reader think will get a good <u>grade</u>.

4. Children don't get good <u>grades</u> on <u>report</u> cards because they are lucky.
5. Good <u>grades</u> mean the child did good work.

C. 1. report   2. grade
    3. card   4. or

D.   What does a good <u>grade</u> on a <u>report</u> <u>card</u> mean? It means the child did a lot of work to get the <u>grade</u>. Some children have trouble giving a <u>report</u>. A parent can help by talking with the child about what to say in the <u>report</u>, or they can spend time reading it together. Soon the child will get good <u>grades</u> on <u>report</u> <u>cards</u>.

▶ **Page 40**

A. <u>scan</u>   <u>skin</u>   <u>slip</u>   <u>smoke</u>
   <u>scold</u>   <u>sky</u>   <u>sled</u>   <u>smell</u>
   <u>snip</u>   <u>spend</u>   <u>stand</u>   <u>swim</u>
   <u>snake</u>   <u>spell</u>   <u>store</u>   <u>sway</u>

B. slay   sky
   stay   sly
   sway   spy

C. 1. spell   2. stay
    3. slip   4. spend
    5. stand

▶ **Page 41**

A. greet, sleet, sweet

B. 1. meet
    2. sweet
    3. greet

C. Dean, Jean, wean

D. 1. Jean
    2. mean
    3. lean

▶ **Page 42**

A. 1. reread   1. unlucky
     2. remind   2. unsold
     3. repay   3. unclear
     4. rerun   4. unloved

B.   Jay thinks he is <u>unlucky</u> to have a teacher who makes him work a lot. But someday he will want to <u>repay</u> her for her help. The teacher tells Jay that he must <u>reread</u> things many times. She makes him <u>redo</u> work that has mistakes in it.

C. 1. unclear   2. remind
     3. undo   4. unloved

▶ **Page 45**

Think About It

Discuss your answers with your instructor.

1. He got a job and quit school.
2. He wants to help his son with his school work.
3. She suggests that he attend reading classes for adults at the school.
4. Summaries should include the idea that Jay's trouble with reading and spelling made Mr. Sanders realize how much he needed to learn to read so he can help his son. Mr. Sanders talks to Jay's teacher and finds out it's not too late to go back to school.

Write About It

Discuss your writing with your instructor.

▶ **Page 46**

A. 1. **b.** he thinks he can get by without reading.
     2. **c.** she has many children to work with.
     3. **b.** Jay's father can help Jay.

B. Parents Are Teachers, Too

▶ **Page 47**

B. 1. Jay made his best grade in math.

2. Jay's worst grade was an *F*. He got an *F* in both reading and spelling.
3. No, Jay doesn't do his work on time. He got an <u>Unsatisfactory</u> on the part of his report card *Turns work in on time*. That's probably part of the reason he got low grades in reading and spelling.

Unit 4

▶ **Page 50**

A. Answers will vary.

B. 1. I gave Maria a (hug) when I learned about our (child).
2. The (doctor) at the (clinic) said our (child) will (come) in June.
3. I'm a (heavy) (smoker), but I (hope) to quit soon for our (child's) sake.

C.

u		d			s	
p	a	r	e	n	t	s
		i			r	
		v			e	
		e			e	
					t	

▶ **Page 51**

B. 1. My wife Maria is doing what the doctor told her.
2. We're learning how to be <u>responsible</u> parents.
3. My <u>wife</u> stopped smoking because it isn't good for the baby.
4. As a mother-to-be, she must think of her health.
5. <u>Responsible</u> parents try to make a good life for children.

C. 1. wife   2. baby
    3. responsible   4. as, as

D.   After my wife found out she was going to have a baby, we both stopped smoking. We're responsible for our baby's health. As our child gets big, we'll feel responsible for the child's schooling as well.

▶ **Page 52**

B. 1. Before you know it, we'll have a new baby.
   2. Do you think the baby will know that I'm a new father?
   3. To be a good father, I must learn many new things.
   4. I need to know how to carry a small child.
   5. What do new parents feed a small baby?

C. 1. Before   2. new
    3. know   4. Small

D.   We have a lot to think about before the baby comes. My wife and I will be responsible for a new life. Does a small child cry all night? Will I need to spend more time at home than I did before? We know our lives are going to be different, but we feel good about a new baby in the family.

▶ **Page 53**

B. 1. Maria's best friend Jan is pregnant, too.
   2. Jan tells Maria that all pregnant women don't feel tired.
   3. She rocks the baby to stop it from crying.
   4. Jan says that new parents may feel tired from getting up late at night to feed the baby.

C. 1. late   2. rock
    3. tired   4. pregnant

D.   Maria was feeling tired, and she went to see the doctor. That was when she found out she is pregnant. I came home late that night, but she was up to tell me the good news. As soon as the baby comes, I want to spend time rocking our baby.

▶ **Page 54**

A. blend   clinic   fly
   blink   clan   flag
   glad   player   sly
   gland   plan   sleet

B. blink   blight
   clink   flight
   plink   plight
   slink   slight

C. 1. plan
   2. plight
   3. glad

▶ **Page 55**

A. block, clock, smock

B. 1. rock   2. smock
    3. clock   4. block

C. plate, skate, state

D. 1. late   2. date
    3. plate   4. rate

▶ **Page 56**

A. 1. families   2. cries
    3. cities   4. tries
    5. countries

B.   Maria's parents and mine were from different countries. Then they came to this country, but they were in different cities. Our families did not meet before our wedding.

C. 1. families   2. cries
    3. babies   4. countries

▶ **Page 59**

Think About It
Discuss your answers with your instructor.

1. Yes. They feel lucky, have told their families, have prepared for the baby's arrival, and have made changes in their own lives (stopped smoking).

2. They will have to rearrange their schedules to see that the baby's needs are met. They may be tired from getting up at night when the baby cries.

3. They'll feed and rock the child and see that the child gets a good education.

4. Summaries should include the idea that Maria and Carlos have done a lot of thinking and planning that will make having a new baby to take care of easier. They are both happy that they are having a child and look forward to being responsible parents.

Write About It
Discuss your writing with your instructor.

▶ **Page 60**
B. 1. Carlos and Maria will be responsible parents.
C. Responsible Parents

▶ **Page 61**
B. 1. Maria should take one tablet daily.
2. Maria should call the drugstore or pharmacy to get more tablets.
3. There are 100 tablets in the bottle. There is 100 beside Qty., or quantity.
4. No, Maria's father should not take the tablets. These tablets may not help him with his problem. He should see his own doctor.

Unit 5

▶ **Page 64**
A. Answers will vary.
B. 1. In (June), my wife and I (took) the family on an outing.
2. We (took) two big (bags) of food, a (tape player) with (tapes), and our (camera).
3. When my wife got out of the (truck), she slipped and landed on her (hip).
C. 1. d 2. a 3. b 4. c

▶ **Page 65**
B. 1. Some friends of mine went to a foreign country this summer.
2. They did not know how to get around and had trouble talking to the people there.
3. As soon as they could get around without much help, my friends saw a lot of the city.
C. 1. Summer   2. foreign
   3. saw   4. around
D.   When my family came to this country, it was a foreign land to them. They did not know how to get around in a big city. They were not used to the hot summers. Things were different for them, but they saw this foreign land as a new chance for a new life.

▶ **Page 66**
B. 1. We found a good cook for the picnic.
2. After we meet the cook, we should thank him for the snacks.
3. When I go to a picnic, I don't mind the bugs.

4. After all, what is a <u>picnic</u> without a big bug or two?

C. 1. picnic   2. cook
    3. thank   4. snacks

D.   This summer we all met for a family <u>picnic</u>. The sun was out all day, and the food looked good. We <u>snacked</u>, played baseball, and talked. My brother was the <u>cook</u> for all the food for the <u>picnic</u>. We <u>thanked</u> him for doing a good job.

▶ **Page 67**

B. 1. Many people go to the <u>park</u> in the summer.
    2. Park rules state people can't walk on the <u>grass</u>.
    3. The children can <u>jump</u> in the lake and swim.
    4. The <u>newcomers</u> sat at a table by us.

C. 1. park   2. newcomers
    3. jump   4. grass

D.   People use the <u>park</u> in different ways. Sometimes they have picnics or swim in the lake. Children like to run around on the dock and <u>jump</u> in the cold water. The <u>park</u> is owned by the city, and the rules the city set up help <u>newcomers</u> to the <u>park</u> know what they should do.

▶ **Page 68**

A. <u>chance</u>   <u>shy</u>   <u>shrug</u>
    <u>child</u>   <u>shake</u>   <u>shrink</u>
    <u>then</u>   <u>thank</u>   <u>when</u>
    <u>that</u>   <u>thing</u>   <u>why</u>

B. chin   shine
    shin   shrine
    thin   whine

C. 1. shine   2. that
    3. shin   4. think

▶ **Page 69**

A. black, shack, stack, track

B. 1. pack
    2. sack
    3. back

C. blank, drank, frank

D. 1. bank
    2. drank
    3. sank

▶ **Page 70**

A. 1. stillness   1. thankful
    2. neatness   2. playful
    3. sadness   3. useful
    4. sickness   4. handful
    5. shyness   5. hopeful

B.   I'm <u>hopeful</u> that we'll have a good day for our picnic. The children will be <u>playful</u> in the park. I've told them to be <u>helpful</u> when we get there. I'm glad that <u>sickness</u> didn't keep the family at home.

C. 1. handful
    2. shyness
    3. thankful

▶ **Page 73**

Think About It

Discuss your answers with your instructor.

    1. He doesn't like them because they are different. He doesn't trust them or want to get to know them.
    2. He thought the man was trying to hurt his son.
    3. Jack did change his mind because he saw the newcomers were not that different. Jack and the newcomer talked, shook hands, and then shared picnic food.

4. Summaries should include the idea that Jack doesn't like people different from himself, but he is beginning to get to know and accept them. Jack and his family don't see many new people in the town where they live, and they will have to get used to newcomers.

Write About It

Discuss your writing with your instructor.

▶ **Page 74**

A. 3, 2, 1

B. I. **b.** before Kate and Jack let them run to the dock.

2. **c.** after the doctor helped Reed.

▶ **Page 75**

B. I. Yes, most parks have rules like these to make the park safe for visitors and to protect the park grounds.

2. The first thing parents should do when they take the family to the park is read the rules and make sure everyone understands them.

3. Rule 1 and Rule 3 have to do with eating or drinking.

4. You might see rules that say no glass, alcohol, or loud music. You might see rules about the use of boats in the lake.

Unit 6

▶ **Page 78**

A. Answers will vary.

B. I. (Sometimes) I have (problems) talking to a (person) I don't know.

2. My (own) (wife) tells me I can be a (fine) (talker), but it (does) not help me.

3. Being in a big group (gives) me a (lonely) feeling.

C.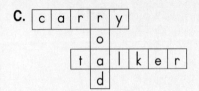

▶ **Page 79**

B. I. I would like to be a <u>better</u> talker.

2. Who can I <u>ask</u> to help me get <u>over</u> this problem?

3. I can <u>ask</u> my friend Fran to help me.

4. I could not <u>ask</u> for a <u>better</u> friend than Fran.

C. I. would   2. ask

3. better   4. over

D. <u>Would</u> you feel lonely in a big group of people? I <u>would</u>. Fran says I'd <u>better</u> learn to talk. <u>Over</u> and <u>over</u> again she tells me this, "Walk around, and soon you'll meet a person who <u>would</u> like to chat."

▶ **Page 80**

B. I. My wife likes to go to <u>every</u> <u>party</u>, big or small.

2. I <u>never</u> want to go to a <u>party</u> where there are lots of people.

3. When I meet new people, I <u>never</u> know what to say.

4. I always feel better when I can <u>bring</u> my wife.

5. For a shy person like me, <u>every</u> <u>party</u> is lonely.

C. I. never   2. every

3. party   4. bring

D. When I'm at a big <u>party</u>, I would like to feel better than I do. <u>Every</u> other person is having a good time, but I'm faking it. Being around people I don't know <u>brings</u> out my shyness. I <u>never</u> know the right thing to say. Does a big <u>party</u> make you feel this way?

▶ **Page 81**

B. 1. My wife's <u>company</u> gives a big party on a holiday.
2. She always asks me to <u>join</u> her friends from work.
3. They talk about people and things from the <u>company</u>.
4. Because I don't know what they are talking about, I feel that I don't <u>belong</u> there.
5. I must learn how to <u>join</u> the <u>club</u>.

C. 1. company   2. belong
3. club   4. join

D. When my wife's <u>company</u> gives a party, I don't have a good time. I feel like I'm on my own—that I don't <u>belong</u> to the group. I don't know how to <u>join</u> in the fun. Why do I feel that they have a <u>club</u> and I don't <u>belong</u> to it?

▶ **Page 82**

A. <u>write</u>   <u>know</u>   <u>guitar</u>   <u>right</u>
<u>wrap</u>   <u>knit</u>   <u>guide</u>   <u>knight</u>

B. knit   wrote
knock   wring
knot   wry
knight   wrap
knee   wren

C. 1. know   2. wring
3. knit   4. wrap
5. right

▶ **Page 83**

A. spring, string, swing, wring

B. 1. swing
2. sing
3. bring

C. grub, shrub, snub

D. 1. club
2. snub
3. hub

▶ **Page 84**

A. St.   Rd.   Dr.   Ave.   oz.   lb.

B. My wife works for the B. D. Clay <u>Co.</u> on Shell <u>Ave.</u> The company has a health plan with <u>Dr.</u> Parker. The doctor works at Pope <u>St.</u> and School <u>Rd.</u> I will see <u>Dr.</u> Parker at the company party on Sunday, June 4.

C. 1. Dr. Key   2. Land Ave.
3. 25 lb.   4. Dean Co.
5. Dune St.   6. 5 oz.
7. Waters Rd.

▶ **Page 87**

Think About It
Discuss your answers with your instructor.
1. He feels shy and uncomfortable, not at ease with people he doesn't know.
2. She is outgoing and at ease in social situations. She talks and laughs with others.
3. She suggests ways he can start a conversation, and ways he can enjoy himself, like playing the guitar or getting people involved in games.
4. Summaries should include the idea that Rick dislikes parties because he is shy, but that after talking with Fran he feels he might be able to overcome his shyness.

Write About It
Discuss your writing with your instructor.

▶ **Page 88**

A. 1. No   2. Yes
B. 1. shy   2. like

Page 89

B. **I.** Sentences 2 and 4 tell you what not to do if you are feeling shy.

    2. Answers will vary.

    3. Many people are shy. There may be other people who are feeling the same way you are.

Unit 7

▶ Page 92

A. Answers will vary.

B. **I.** I would like to (learn) a (responsible) job and (join) a big (company).

    2. I know I need to (learn) more about how to look for a good job.

    3. I'll look (over) the (want) ads, ask (around), and make a (list) of where to look.

    4. I might need to think about going (back) to (school).

C. **I.** join   **2.** learn

    3. new   **4.** list

▶ Page 93

B. **I.** The city runs the learning <u>center</u>.

    2. Bill has worked at the <u>center</u> for a <u>year</u>.

    3. He <u>keeps</u> telling me I need a <u>year</u> of school.

    4. I should try going back to school <u>now</u>.

C. **I.** keep   **2.** now

    3. center   **4.** year

D.   Bill has been at the <u>center</u> for a <u>year</u> <u>now</u>. He can go to school and work at the same time. He <u>keeps</u> trying to get me to come in and talk to someone at the <u>center</u>. Maybe <u>now</u> that my job with Jill is over I will. Now is a good time of year to begin over.

▶ Page 94

B. **I.** <u>Once</u> you get into the center, you make money as you <u>train</u>.

    2. This school is different from the ones I <u>once</u> went to.

    3. The people at the center ask about <u>your</u> skills and what you like to do.

    4. I'm glad Bill made me <u>listen</u> to him.

C. **I.** train   **2.** Your

    3. listen   **4.** Once

D.   Bill said, "<u>Listen</u>, the center can help you. You can <u>train</u> for a job and go to school at the same time. The city has joined together with companies that <u>train</u> people. <u>Once</u> you get into the center, they <u>listen</u> to <u>your</u> job needs, and then get you a job. You make money as you learn and <u>train</u>."

▶ Page 95

B. **I.** I wanted to begin a <u>career</u> at Jill's shop.

    2. She saw that I was <u>careful</u> with the TV sets and radios.

    3. Some days I worked <u>straight</u> from 8 A.M. to 6 P.M.

    4. I didn't get to meet many of Jill's <u>customers</u>.

C. **I.** straight   **2.** customers

    3. careful   **4.** career

D.   On my first day at the center, I was sent <u>straight</u> to Mr. Teller at his shop. His <u>customers</u> have car radios, TVs, and CD players they bring in. Mr. Teller looked <u>straight</u> at me. He told me if I'm as <u>careful</u> as he thinks I am, I can do well in this <u>career</u>.

▶ **Page 96**

A.
1. wh(y)
2. m(y)
3. b(y)
4. dr(y)

1. luck(y)
2. carr(y)
3. part(y)
4. lonel(y)

B.
1. sly
2. try
3. cry
4. fly

1. baby
2. healthy
3. many
4. heavy

C. I've had <u>many</u> jobs over the years. I'm <u>lucky</u> to have a chance to (try) a new school. I don't know (why) (my) old school didn't work for me. Now I can train for a good career and make <u>money</u> at the same time.

▶ **Page 97**

A. sheep, sleep, steep, sweep

B.
1. keep
2. steep
3. deep

C. clear, shear, smear, spear

D.
1. near
2. hear
3. clear

▶ **Page 98**

A. Sun., Mon., Tues., Wed., Thurs., Fri., Sat.

B. Jan., Feb., Mar., Apr., Aug., Sept., Oct., Nov., Dec.

C. It was a cold <u>Monday</u> in <u>December</u> when I saw "For Rent" on Jill's store. I went to look for a job on <u>Wednesday</u>, <u>Thursday</u>, and <u>Friday</u>. All the people said, "We have no work for you. Try again in <u>January</u>, <u>February</u>, or <u>March</u>." On <u>Saturday</u> and <u>Sunday</u> I sat home and moped, but I'll try again on <u>Monday</u>.

▶ **Page 101**
Think About It
Discuss your answers with your instructor.

1. He was surprised that part of his class schedule included three days a week at a job, that he was paid for his work, that he also had to attend reading classes, that he was graded on his work.

2. He wanted to learn more about TV repair than he had learned at Jill's. He wanted to be able to work with customers and take care of their repair problems. He felt this was his chance to make a career with a good company.

3. He improved his reading skills so that he could learn how to practice different skills.

4. Summaries should include the idea that Jim was tired of going from job to job, so he went back to school to get on-the-job training and improve his basic reading and math skills to start a career in TV repair.

Write About It
Discuss your writing with your instructor.

▶ **Page 102**

B. Fact 1: Fay was in training for a new job.
Fact 2: Fay got paid if she did good work or not.
Fact 3: She was sometimes late for work.
Fact 4: Her boss didn't ask her to stay when the training was over.

C. 1. Fay is not in the right job.

▶ **Page 103**

B.
1. **a.** 8:00 A.M.   **b.** 4:00 P.M.
2. **a.** 1:00 P.M.   **b.** 3:00 P.M.
3. She works at the Customer Desk.
4. Workers are scheduled for different work times so someone will always be there to work at the Customer Desk.

Unit 1 Review

▶ **Page 104**

A. 1. elected   2. horse ranch, jewelry
    3. Native American   4. again

B. 1. make   1. lovely
   2. luck   2. letter
   3. worked   3. silver
   4. puts   4. congress

C. 1. lovely   2. nightly   3. needy

Unit 2 Review

▶ **Page 105**

A. 1. coupons   2. could
   3. roommate   4. think

B. 1. why; why   2. drink, dry; drink
   3. try; try   4. think; think

C. 1. sold   2. paid   3. made, spent

Unit 3 Review

▶ **Page 106**

A. 1. always   2. grades
   3. means   4. must, after

B. 1. meet, mean; meet   2. greet; greet
   3. Jean; Jean   4. meet, mean; mean

C. 1. unclear   2. reread
   3. remind   4. unlucky

Unit 4 Review

▶ **Page 107**

A. 1. wife   2. responsible
   3. Before   4. new

B. 1. plate; plate   2. block; block
   3. late, lock; late   4. rate, rock; rock

C. babies, families, cries, countries

1. families   2. cries
3. babies   4. countries

Unit 5 Review

▶ **Page 108**

A. 1. park   2. newcomers
   3. around   4. jump

B. 1. pack; pack   2. back, bank; back
   3. thank; thank   4. back, bank; bank

C. 1. thankful   2. goodness   3. helpful

Unit 6 Review

▶ **Page 109**

A. 1. never   2. would
   3. belong   4. Every

B. 1. club, cling; club   2. snub; snub
   3. swing; swing   4. bring; bring

C. 1. Street —— oz.
   2. pound —— Dr.
   3. Avenue —— St.
   4. ounces —— Ave.
   5. Doctor —— lb.

Unit 7 Review

▶ **Page 110**

A. 1. center   2. train
   3. now   4. customers

B. 1. year; year   2. dear, deep; Dear
   3. near; near   4. keep; keep

C. 1. Wednesday —— Dec.
   2. February —— Apr.
   3. Tuesday —— Thurs.
   4. December —— Wed.
   5. Thursday —— Tues.
   6. April —— Feb.

Word List

● ● ● ● ●

Below is a list of the 350 words that are presented to students in *Book Four* of *Reading for Today*. These words are introduced on sight word, phonics, language, comprehension, and life skills pages. The words will be reviewed in later books. Students should also be familiar with other words based on the phonetically regular spellings of long and short vowel sounds in the consonant-vowel-consonant (CVC) and consonant-vowel-consonant + silent *e* (CVC + *e*) patterns.

A
after
again
ago
always
Apr.
April
around
as
ask
assignment
attention
Aug.
August
Ave.
avenue

B
babies
baby
back
bank
bashful
bean
been
beet
before
began
begin
belong
best
better
black
blank
blend
blight

blink
block
bottle
bought
brag
brand
bring
brink

C
card
career
careful
center
chin
cities
clan
clean
clear
clink
clock
club
Co.
company
complaint
Congress
cook
cost
could
countries
coupon
cream
cries
crop
cry
customer

D
daily
date
Dean
dear
Dec.
December
deep
differently
Dr.
drank
drink
drip
drop
drug
dry

E
elected
enjoy
every
expiration

F
families
fear
Feb.
February
feet
first
flag
flight
fly
foreign
found
fray

Fri.
Friday
friendly
fry

G
gate
glad
gland
goodness
government
grade
grass
gray
greet
grip
grub
guide

H
handful
handy
healthy
hear
helpful
here
hilly
hopeful
horse
hub

I
invite

J
Jan.
January
Jean
jeep
jewelry
join
July
jump

K
keep
king
knee
knight
knit
knock
knot
know

L
late
law
lb.
lean
learned
less
letter
lifeguard
likely
list
listen
lock
longer
lovely
lunch

M
Mar.
March
math
May
mean
meet
mighty
mock
Mon.
Monday
most
much
must

N
name
Native American
near
neatness
needy
never
new
newcomers
nightly
Nov.
November
now

O
Oct.
October
once
or
other
ounce
over
owner
oz.

P
pack
paid
park

party
picnic
pink
plan
plate
playful
plight
plink
pound
pregnant
put

R
ranch
rancher
rate
Rd.
redo
relax
remember
remind
repay
report
reread
rerun
responsible
ring
rink
rock
roommate
rub

S
sack
sadness
safely
sank
Sat.
Saturday
save
saved
saw
scan

schedule
school
scold
Senate
senator
Sept.
September
shack
shear
sheep
shin
should
shrine
shrink
shrub
shrug
shy
shyness
sickness
signature
silver
sing
sink
skate
skin
sky
slay
sled
sleep
sleet
slight
slink
slip
sly
small
smear
smell
smock
snack
snake
snip
snub
sock

soon
spell
spend
spent
spring
spy
St.
stack
state
stay
steep
stillness
straight
strap
stray
string
strip
summer
Sun.
Sunday
sway
sweep
sweet
swim
swing

T
tablet
taught
thank
thankful
then
thin
think
thought
Thurs.
Thursday
time
tired
too
track
train
tray

tries
trip
try
tub
Tues.
Tuesday

U
unclear
undo
unloved
unlucky
unsold
useful

W
wean
Wed.
Wednesday
weep
where
which
whine
why
wife
wing
wink
word
worst
would
wrap
wren
wring
write
wrote
wry

Y
year
your